Kinascu by

Surrender doesn't have to be a bad word and Kris Camealy shows us why. Not only does she offer an honest, practical narrative on her own experience with the power of surrender, she also casts a hopeful vision for those of us who struggle with holding on, micromanaging, and over-performing our way through life. What an important book!

EMILY P. FREEMAN, *Wall Street Journal* bestselling author of *The Next Right Thing*

Kris Camealy is a guide for modern-day pilgrims who are desperate for meaning and good meals. If you feel lost in your own story, she will walk you into hers so that you can understand the twists and turns. And come face to face with a faith that she openly admits can some days feel like a maze. Then she will walk you back out again, a woman who takes God seriously enough to argue with him and is just as comfortable in church as she is with her cast iron skillet. In other words, she's worth trusting.

LISA-JO BAKER, bestselling author of *Never Unfriended* and cohost of the Out of the Ordinary Podcast.

Most of us come to surrender slantwise and obstinate, forced into it by unwanted and unforeseen circumstances. As a fellow traveler through the wilderness, Kris Camealy comes at surrender differently, as one who has been pursued and embraced by love. *Everything is Yours* is an invitation to experience God's heart and be surprised by joy in the uncertain times of life. Accept and you are sure to be inspired and changed by it.

SHELLY MILLER, Author of *Rhythms of Rest: Finding the Spirit of Sabbath in a Busy World*

God desires all of who I am to be fully surrendered to him. But on most days its as if I'm holding onto my plans, fears, or insecurities with one hand while holding onto Jesus with my other hand. *Everything is Yours* has helped me to finally let go of these things; helping me place both of my arms around the neck of Jesus as I live out his designs for my life. This is not a book full of burdensome bullet points, but an honest, grace-filled conversation that helps once-divided hearts to wholeheartedly reconnect to the God who longs for their enduring embrace.

TRACY STEEL, speaker and author of *A Redesigned Life*

Clear, rich with stories, and deep with reflections on the nature of surrender, Kris Camealy has given us a gift that is worth returning to over and over again. Her devotional writing is among the best I know of in the church today.

ED CYZEWSKI, author of *Flee, Be Silent, Pray and Reconnect: Spiritual Restoration from Digital Distraction*

In *Everything Is Yours*, Kris Camealy's story of her own slow surrender becomes a window through which we get to look at God and see His goodness and tenderness. We also get to see what obedience looks like in one ordinary life—the struggles and mistakes, the attempted bargains, the flat-out refusals, the oh-fine-have-it-your-ways. Kris knows how hard it is to let go of all the things we clutch in our tight little fists, how grievous that can be. But she also knows that on the other side of that grief—is freedom and joy. And she gently guides our gaze back again and again to Jesus, the author and perfecter of our faith. Compelling and readable, *Everything Is Yours* is an invitation to move deeper into the heart of God, the only place we know true freedom and joy.

K.C.IRETON, author of *The Circle of Seasons: Meeting God in the Church Year*

Having recently come kicking and screaming through my own season of surrender, I can assure you that Kris Camealy writes the unvarnished truth in this book without sugarcoating words, without tiptoeing around the topic and without coddling her reader. Instead she boldly confronts both the pain and promise of surrender with refreshing candor and authenticity, confidently leading the reader through the labyrinth of spiritual transformation toward true freedom. If you are ready once and for all to say "yes" to true surrender, if you are ready to accept the invitation into deeper intimacy with God, you can count 100 percent on Kris Camealy and

Everything Is Yours to be your trusted guides every step of the way.

MICHELLE DERUSHA, author of *True You: Letting Go of Your False Self to Uncover the Person God Created*

Everything is Yours is not a book I thought I needed to read. However, a few short pages in, I found it a book I wanted to read and, despite my initial impression, desperately needed to. It's a humbling thing to find oneself convicted, yet gently and lovingly named on page after page of reading. Such is a good book that evokes tears and prayers. As Kris Camealy says within these pages, "...surrender does have a cost. Saying 'yes' to God's plans and purposes over our own is a risky thing. We will be changed by this kind of obedience." Yes, please. As long as I have breath, Lord, keep conforming me into the image of Christ. *Everything is Yours* is a tender companion on the continued journey of sanctification. A must-read for those who, like me, continually discover the need for surrender—over and over and over again.

LAURA J. BOGGESS, author of *Playdates with God: Having a Childlike faith in a Grown-Up World*

I have had some deep conversations with Kris Camealy, and each time I come away with my spirit refreshed. I also come away challenged. Reading *Everything Is Yours* is a similar experience—it's like having an enlightening and honest conversation with a sister. A sister who asks hard questions of you. But not without first asking them of herself. Like, how many of God's gifts have you missed because of your resistance to surrender? Kris, in revealing her own struggle to surrender her expectations, plans, dreams, (and her whole heart), lovingly brings us to the feet of Jesus and says, "Let go of all of it—the whats and the whys—so you can cling to the Who…so you can know the utter freedom of proclaiming, 'Everything is Yours. I am Yours!'

AMANDA CLEARY EASTEP, Sr. Developmental Editor, Moody Publishers

There is a cadence that marks the convergence of wisdom and

wordcraft. It sings softly but sounds crystal clear. It rings without fanfare yet ripples into our thinking and into our souls. It stirs wakefulness and heralds transformation. Not many books are so marked. This one is. Read it, in a sense, at your peril. Read it and be called. Read it and be known. Read it and be free.

LANCIA E. SMITH Founder of *Cultivating* and *The Cultivating Project*

Kris weaves story and Scripture together in a way that invites us all to see past her writing and into the heart of the one true Author. Her latest book, *Everything Is Yours*, powerfully and purely extends an earnest appeal for a deep dive into those places we often prefer to keep hidden, masked by the familiar phrases and motions of the modern practice of Christian faith. As she uncovers the layers of her own self-sufficiency, we are the beneficiaries of new awareness of the ways our self-fueled faith has wrapped around our own hearts. Offering no step-by-step guidelines, Kris has gifted us something far more valuable—a careful removal of the hope that we're getting it right, replacing it with the real and only hope we have in Christ, revealed through His Word. You'll find yourself undone once again by familiar pieces of Scripture, eyes wide open to the promise of abundant life found only in the Person of Christ.

TERI LYNNE UNDERWOOD, author of *Praying for Girls: Asking God for the Things They Need Most*

In her newest book, *Everything is Yours*, Kris Camealy offers readers a compelling collection of personal stories, carefully chosen scripture and eloquent prayers centered on the theme of surrendering one's life more fully to God. With a tone of both tenderness and strong conviction, Kris walks readers through deeply important questions regarding Christian theology and a believer's personal decisions of living a more life fully surrendered. Read *Everything Is Yours* slowly and thoughtfully, perhaps with as a devotional or personal study. Read it with a small group and dig deeper into the questions and thoughts that bubble up. Either way read *Everything Is Yours* and move closer to a life fully surrendered to the will of God.

ELIZABETH WYNNE MARSHALL, Poet and Host of *Peabiddies Podcast*

Kris Camealy has written a book on surrender, but not without first becoming intimately acquainted with what it means to lay down her own life. In page after page she unpacks the truth about God's call on our lives and then shows us what that means from her own. The image that stood out most poignantly to me was her two-year-old daughter in her green-footed pajamas praying with her face flat to the floor. I'll never sing "I Surrender All" the same way again.

CHARITY SINGLETON CRAIG, author of *The Art of the Essay: From Ordinary Life to Extraordinary Words*

When you open the pages of Everything Is Yours, you're unearthing a treasure. Kris Camealy writes with a soul-stirring depth and urgency that will have you contemplating your own faith in important ways. She's an engaging storyteller who invites you into her own life in order to point you to God. Excellent writing that had me both wanting to linger on each page and race to the end, this book deserves a place on bookshelves everywhere!

ROBIN DANCE, author of *Born to Wander: Why Knowing God is Better Than Knowing it All*

Compelling and convicting! Kris Camealy challenges us to consider the true state of our hearts—and determine daily to surrender more fully to God, that we might experience a deeper, richer relationship with Him.

CHRISTIN DITCHFIELD, author of *What Women Should Know About Letting It Go: Breaking Free from Guilt, Discouragement, and Defeat*

Everything Is Yours

Everything Is Yours

How Giving God Your Whole Heart Changes Your Whole Life

KRIS CAMEALY

REFINE *Media*

REFINE *Media*

EVERYTHING IS YOURS

ISBN 978-1-7342839-0-7

eBook ISBN 978-1-7342839-1-4

Printed in the United States of America

Published in the United States by Refine Media, LLC, Westerville, OH

260 W. State Street, Box 1113 Westerville, OH, 43065

http://refineretreat.com/refine-media

www.kriscamealy.com

Cover design by Kris Camealy / Cover art background image by Christine Hiester
shapingtheriver.com

"Believing in him is not the same as believing things about him such as that he was born of a virgin and raised Lazarus from the dead. Instead, it is a matter of giving our hearts to him, of come hell or high water putting our money on him, the way a child believes in a mother or a father, the way a mother or a father believes in a child."

Frederick Buechner

Contents

Dear Reader,

I have told people it's taken me five years to write this book, and if we're speaking about honest-to-goodness effort, pen-to-paper, or fingers-to-keyboard, then that's true. But when I try to remember how it actually all began, I have to go back further than the last five years. Before I could write it, I had to live it. Or more specifically, I needed to wrestle with God about it. After all, this is a book about surrender, and I am still learning what that means.

Seven years ago, a mentor asked me, "If your life were a book, what would it be called?" I remember hesitating only a moment before answering her: "Holey, Wholly, Holy, as in, holey—being broken and in need of God, wholly—becoming fully surrendered to God, and holy—being sanctified by God's refining love." That same year I wrote a small book by that title. That book was an act of obedience. That book was an altar of worship and remembrance—a thing marking an encounter with God. Ever since then, my journey with Jesus has looked nothing like it did before. In writing that book I told God that I was willing—willing to do whatever thing He asked me to, no matter how uncomfortable or difficult. That was probably closer to the real beginning of this book. That was the first time I remember really surrendering my own desires for God's purposes. If you've ever told God that you were willing to do whatever He asked of you, you know how faithful He is to invite you to new spaces of obedience, new levels of surrender. And if you haven't told God such a thing, then I pray that by the time you turn the last page of this book, you do. It is the only way to live a truly free life.

The words authenticity and vulnerability have gotten a bit of overplay in our current culture. We roll our eyes a little at these words. We've seen the over-sharer bare their soul in the name of being vulnerable, and felt the assault of too much personal information. That said, authenticity and vulnerability are a big deal to me. I confess, I take small pride in my ability to sniff out a phony, and because I value authenticity in others, I hold myself to the same standard. This is not a highlight reel of my perfectly surrendered life. Some of the stories I share here do not reflect my finest moments. But these imperfect attempts at giving God room to act are the windows through which God's light has broken through. For that reason, I vulnerably offer them up in hopes that you will catch a glimpse of His back, as He passes between the rocks and hard places (Exodus 33:22).

I am not a biblical scholar. I am, in church terms, a layperson, a practitioner of faith. I speak only as someone close to the ground, learning as I go, like the rest of most of us. I have not graduated from this class. I am a perpetual freshman. And this book is not a how-to manual on surrender. I stubbornly resist 3- or 5-step methodology writing, even though I concede it is sometimes the most efficient way to make a point. I concede it, but I do not practice it. Years ago, I stopped asking God for the bullet-point version outlining how to live the life of faith. I think we were both relieved. Surrender is deeply personal and will look different in all of our lives. But if you insist on a bullet point method for how to become what Paul calls "a living sacrifice" (Romans 12:1), I've only got one bullet—Pray to become a living sacrifice.

Remember that terrible old proverbial statement, "God helps those who help themselves"? This appears exactly nowhere in Scripture. God sent His Son Jesus to earth precisely because we, try-as-we-might, cannot help ourselves in the way of salvation. Instead of us working towards that end, God reaches down into the muck of our lives and grabs hold of our hearts, drawing us towards Himself. Thus, this book is not a self-help book. Rather, this book is for those of us who have tried and failed miserably to help ourselves. It simply doesn't work. I love the way Eugene Peterson's translation of Romans 12:1 frames this idea of a surrendered life:

So here's what I want you to do, God helping you: Take your everyday, ordinary life—your sleeping, eating, going-to-work, and walking-around life—and place it before God as an offering. Embracing what God does for you is the best thing you can do for him.

Take it all. Place it all. Embrace it all. For everything is His. Our whole lives. Every moment—all of it belongs to God. Each of the chapters in this book concludes with a prayer. Make the prayers your own. Stick your name in there, and speak the words from your own heart in a way that feels true to how you communicate with God. Then, even if it feels untrue, believe that God will meet you where you are. Fists clenched or open—whatever, however. He's willing to take us whatever way we stumble towards Him.

By His strength, for His glory,

Kris

1

Comfortable Deceptions

It sounds terribly cliché, but I don't suppose any of us decides our come-to-Jesus moment. We don't get to plan our Damascus road conversions.

Jen Pollock Michel

"She's lucky. It could have been worse." That's what the doctors said.

It was a sunny Saturday afternoon, a perfect day for riding bikes which was exactly what my older sister was doing when she careened headfirst into a neighbor's mailbox. Maybe somebody hollered her name. Maybe she turned her head to look at something. Whatever the distraction was, it left its mark when with head turned, she smashed into a neighbor's mailbox. The impact knocked her backwards off her bike onto the pavement. My sister laid there at the base of the curb, her body racked with involuntary, seizure-like convulsions. I ran to find my parents. Dad had been outside, mid-stride with his hands on the mower, and from somewhere in the house my mother emerged, white-faced and panicked. The whole scene happened in an instant. But I recall it as a slow-motion dream. After a trip to the hospital emergency room, my sister spent the next few days shuffling between the couch and her bed, recovering from a severe concussion. It could have been worse. She was lucky.

Decades later, the nightmare of my sister's bike accident revisits me one afternoon when my Mother calls to tell me that my sister is on the brink of hospitalization. As my mom offers up what little details she had in that moment, the memory of my sister's bike accident unfolds slowly, like petals, blossoming into some terrible bloom. In my mind, I see her falling in slow motion, back onto the street. She hits, she falls. She hits, she falls. The scene repeats itself while I struggle to listen to my mother describing the current situation. I fight to keep my composure while my children chatter to each other in the back seat of the van. I glance in my rearview mirror at them, wiping my eyes and holding back a howl fighting its way up from my belly. This time, it's worse. She'll need more than a couple of afternoons on the couch to recover.

Following in my Father's footsteps, my sister and younger brother joined the military right out of college. But not me. I would not serve my country in this way. My refusal to carry this particular family torch boiled down to my resistance to being told what to do. Even this is a gross understatement. In those days, I abhorred being "bossed" and the idea of boot camp or taking orders made me cringe. My fierce sense of independence forbade me from assuming a position in which I would not be the one issuing orders. I lived as if I could handle life on my own. I didn't need anyone to do for me what I could do for myself. This is a painful admission, and not one I share with any sense of pride. This was me before. This was the "old man" me (Ephesians 4:22).

But back to my sister. In 2003, my sister went on to serve the first of two long tours in Iraq. She returned from the war a decorated soldier, earning two bronze stars for her service. But as it turned out, her medals were not the only souvenirs of her tours in the Middle East. She also carried home a broken heart riddled with hidden shrapnel that threatened to tear her apart. My mother called that day, to let me know my sister had raised her white flag. She could not fight it any longer on her own. She surrendered.

Oddly enough, my sister's cry for help revealed a new twist in my own journey. It knocked me off my feet. Moments like this blindside us. These kinds of emotional upheavals most often come without warning, interrupting our everyday rhythms and routines as they force their way into our lives. We can't avoid dealing with them. We don't get to choose our personal tragedies.

"We don't get to cherry pick our come-to-Jesus moments."[1]

Of course, it's these moments that find us out. In the thick of grief, loss and assault, our gods are tested. Here, our comfortable deceptions are confronted. When our souls are assailed with hardship, we cry out to God, but in our pleas, we often assign our own expectations, our own prescriptions for how we expect God to act. We want to be saved, but on our own terms. We want God to move, but only in the direction we're attempting to shove Him, and at the speed that most suits our time-table. It's in these seasons of struggle that we encounter what author Bob Sorge describes as God using the "fire of circumstances mixed with the fire of His word"[2] to uproot our wayward theologies. God always hears our prayers, but He doesn't always answer according to our desires. Trials are a means through which God refines us. Heartbreak is a holy crucible for transformation. I prayed for God to heal my sister. He eventually did. But not before His mercy split me down the center, exposing my own heart disease. While I spent months praying fitful, resentful prayers on behalf of her private suffering, God systematically stripped me down to my bones, smashing my beloved idols one-by-one.

The god of self-sufficiency—smash!
The god of pride—smash!
The god of my own independence—smash!

For months, it seemed that the more I prayed for my sister's recovery, the more God wrenched and tugged at the festering garbage I'd harbored in my own heart.

Perhaps you have experienced this kind of unwelcome awakening. Maybe you're in the middle of a refining season like this right now. You pray for others but it feels more like God is at work in you, than in their lives. We're trying to redirect His attention to the one in need, all the while oblivious, or in denial, about our own desperate necessity. Now that God had my full attention, He went to work on my own heart. This is what happens in a crisis, isn't it? It's like when you're driving with heavy eyelids, only to be suddenly snapped wide awake when your car begins to shudder violently, as you drift across the rumble strips on to the shoulder of the highway. That jarring feeling of realizing how close you were to crashing makes most of us sit up straighter in our seats, maybe roll the window down, taking in large gulps of fresh air. Our senses now pricked with the fear of potential collision, we open our eyes wider than seems natural, and if we're smart, we look for a place to pull over. We're in no condition to keep going like this. We're lucky. It could have been worse.

This desperate season woke me from a deep soul-sleep. I didn't know all of the ways I had been going through the motions in my faith—mouthing the prayers, singing along to worship songs, and yet living in my own strength, following my own agenda, dangerously unaware of the various ways I had yet to surrender my life, my identity—my whole self to God. I'll say more about this as this book unfolds. Actually, that's what this entire book is about.

My sister's call for help saved us both. The difference was she knew she needed it. I had been oblivious.

Comfortable Deceptions

These moments of a sharpened awareness of our own fragility come as an invitation. It's here, in the thick of trouble, where we can experience God's presence. There are always questions. Are we paying attention? Are we listening? Are we willing to let God all the way into our hearts and our circumstances?

I had not been.

The ways we deceive ourselves are as numerous and individual as we are. Many of us will eagerly say that we trust God, but our fretful prayers and worried mumblings reflect the truer situation of our hearts. We pray but lie awake at night working through what-if's. We confess in our creeds that we believe in resurrection, but we live with a perspective of death as a finality, forgetting that death is only a doorway. We confess with our lips that we believe that by our admission of sin, we are forgiven, yet we flog ourselves with harsh self-talk about the ways we continue to fall short. God keeps no record of our wrongs (1 Corinthians 13:5), still our journals teem with lament over our shortcomings.

We profess belief in God's sovereignty while we simultaneously maneuver and manipulate situations and people in order to achieve the outcome we desire. We say "God is in control!" But we live as if we bear sole responsibility for circumstances clearly beyond our ability. I had inadvertently slipped into a mindset of imagining that I was somehow responsible for not only my own life, but my sister's as well. My prayers for her healing sounded more like me issuing orders for how God should act on her behalf.

"How can you ask Him to answer a prayer only the way you want it answered?"[3] My sister's struggle revealed the rotten core of my own self-help faith. The screeching halt of her world simultaneously slammed on the brakes in my own life. It didn't matter that she was living a thousand miles from me at the time. I felt the jerking shudder of my life-as-I-knew-it grinding to a smoking halt. The self-salvation and bootstrap faith I'd been living was no match for the situation we were facing as a family. I had to raise my white flag too. I had to surrender. "Sometimes we try so hard. We push, we shove, we shout, we declare, we say every prayer we know. And all we do is wear ourselves out." [4]

In her book, *Teach Us to Want*, Jen Pollock Michel writes, "At the core of every project of self-salvation is the staunch unwillingness to believe that God's love and forgiveness can be unmerited…It is never easy to live as indebted." A surrendered heart fully admits that it cannot, and must not, do in its own strength. Surrendered living is the epitome of living as one indebted. What I didn't know in those moments with my mother relaying the terrible news to me on the phone, was that I was days away from a head-on collision with grace. God would use this moment to teach me what it looked like to let go.

Brennan Manning had a term for people like me. He referred to those of us Christians who bootstrap our way through life as "practicing Pelagians."[5] In other words, people confident that they can accomplish any task by our own concerted effort.

How many of us would admit that we place more stock in our own behavior and ability than in God's divine intervention and presence in our lives? How many of us resist grace because we believe we are acting in humility? How much pride must we actually assume, if we can look to our heavenly Father and say "no" to His gift? Do we even really know what it means to truly depend on God—what it means to be fully surrendered to Him? Scripture reminds us that God doesn't need our help—that we actually are incapable of giving Him anything, because He made everything:

The God who made the world and everything in it, being Lord of heaven and earth, does not live in temples made by man, nor is he served by human hands, as though he needed anything, since he himself gives to all mankind life and breath and everything.

Acts 17:24-25

It's not our help God wants, but our hearts.

My Will Be Done

In 2005, Sociologists Christian Smith and Melinda Lundquist Denton coined the term "Moralistic Therapeutic Deism," which is essentially, the theology of people who believe:'

- God exists and created and ordered the world
- He watches over His creation
- God wants good behavior from people
- The main goal in life is the achievement of personal happiness
- God doesn't intervene except when truly necessary
- Morally upstanding people go to heaven when they die.

This term wasn't around when I was younger, but it's an apt definition for the theology I grew up with. For many of us, "surrendered living" is little more than a Christian catch phrase. We sing songs like "I Surrender All," but most of us surrender less than all, or maybe even not at all. We don't want to be indebted to anyone. It's uncomfortable. It's countercultural. We might lose friends. We might be misunderstood. It costs us something. Maybe, everything.

"Present your bodies as a living sacrifice, holy and acceptable to God."

Romans 12:1

The Apostle Paul calls this our true worship—to give God all of us—our very selves—as a living sacrifice.

What does that mean?

What does that look like?

Can we honestly say we are living as Romans 12 describes? In his book, *Maximum Faith*, George Barna noted that just 3% of self-professing Christians in America have come to a place where they can say that they have fully surrendered control of their lives to God.[6] *Three Percent.*

I wonder, in this moment, what would we say about ourselves?

Which percentile would our lives place us in? How are we so far off the mark?

Not just the church I grew up in, but the culture I live in proclaims the almighty goodness of autonomy, living for self, in our own strength, and for our own good pleasure and self-glorification. We see this idea so much we may not even be aware of the ways it pervades our thinking. For forty years, a well-recognized fast food chain encouraged and endorsed this concept through their catchy slogan "Have it your way." And so we have, and we do. Before my sister's struggle came to the surface, this message had been the proclamation of my days, the underlying narrative that seeped quietly into my actions and heart.

For many of us "my way" is the mantra of our inner hearts. We want what we want, when we want it, and how we want it. Worse still, this way of thinking leads us to believe we deserve to have what we want. This fast food chain didn't invent this slogan, but only put words around the condition of human desire since the Garden of Eden. If you've read Genesis, you've heard this slogan before.

Did God actually say, 'You shall not eat of any tree in the garden'?" And the woman said to the serpent, "We may eat of the fruit of the trees in the garden, but God said, 'You shall not eat of the fruit of the tree that is in the midst of the garden, neither shall you touch it, lest you die.'" But the serpent said to the woman, "You will not surely die. For God knows that when you eat of it your eyes will be opened, and you will be like God, knowing good and evil."

Genesis 3:1-3

You can have it your way, the serpent hissed. You don't have to do it the way God has said. This has been the bitter cry of creation since the first taste of the forbidden fruit. But the idea of having life our way, while enticing, is counter to the gospel narrative of Jesus, the God-man who came not to be served, but to serve (Matthew 20:28), not to do His will in His way, but to do the will of the Father who sent Him (John 6:38). Even for Jesus, surrender wasn't done according to His purpose, but according to God's. Why should we imagine that for us it is any different? Why should we presume that any other posture will turn out less destructive and despairing than Eve's own insistence on having it her way?

Every time I insist on my own terms and conditions, I step into the chasm that separates me from God—my willful, self-absorbed expectations always reflect the sinful state of my heart. You can't bend when you're standing stiff-kneed.

We live and relive seasons like this—burdened with expectations, clutching in our own strength at an outcome we insist is the right one. Our pride causes us to forget our blindness. We forget that we're operating with a limited scope of the bigger picture. We cannot see what God sees. We are forced to trust Him, to believe that His grace is sufficient, regardless of what our human eyes tell us. Surrender feels too risky to us. Andrew Murray wrote, "Just as a servant knows that he must first obey his master in all things, so the surrender to an implicit and unquestionable obedience must become the essential characteristic of our lives."[7]

God, we hear and read a lot of things that shape our view of You and the world we live in. Some of it's good, and some of it only sounds good, but in practice and application will not lead us into the Promised Land we envision—and to complicate matters, we aren't always keen to make the distinction, between the good, and the sounds-good-but-aren't, ideas. We want what we want, even when it's not what You want for us. That doesn't make a lot of sense, but it's our daily fight, and it's the reason we need Your help. It's the reason we need You. Open our eyes, God. Help us to see the foolishness of living life on our own terms. Everything is yours. Give us the courage to open our hands to You. Replace the lies we've been taught, tricked into, and peer-pressured into believing, with the Truth. Help us to come to know You as You really are, so that we might willingly become that "living sacrifice" that Paul talks about in Your Word.

In Jesus' name, Amen.

2

How Much Does It Cost?

Everything that has value has its price.

Gertrude Lawrence

I'll never forget November 16th, 2004. As a first-time Mom, I had dutifully read and memorized the protocol for properly exposing your toddler to peanuts. Strapping Luke into his highchair, I spread before him a few bits of cracker, placing a pea-sized amount of creamy peanut butter onto the corner of one of the crackers. Always the good eater, he eagerly reached for the snack and began to sample the sweet brown dollop with the tip of his tongue. I stood just steps away, at the sink washing dishes, watching him carefully for any sign of allergic reaction. After a brief minute, I noticed a small red spot near his top lip. It was so small, barely noticeable at first. It looked like a tiny mosquito bite, or as if he had rubbed the edge of his lip. I mentally noted the size and color of the mark. Maybe he'd simply scraped the rough edge of the cracker against his lip. I glanced down at the soapy dish in my hand and then again at my son. Already the red mark was larger, resembling something more like a hive. My hands went cold. Putting the dish in the drying rack, I crossed the kitchen to his high chair. It had maybe been three minutes tops since I'd set him up with his sample, but already, his top lip had swollen to twice its usual size.

Oh Jesus no, I gasped. Sometimes it's not fight-or-flight but a strange combination of both. *Move, Kris, move now. Let's go, Kris, Move! Get him out of the highchair. Get your keys—where are the car keys? Grab your purse, get your phone. Call the pediatrician. Tell them what's happening. Oh! his face is swelling so much! Ask them where to go— tell the nurse where you are, and how far the emergency room is from here. Tell them you are coming now. Is he breathing?*

By the time we arrived at the front desk of the pediatric office, my sons face had swollen so much so that you could no longer see his brown eyes—only two creases on his face where his eyes were usually visible. I'd held it somewhat together until then, but then I lost it. I handed my boy to the doctor who quickly ushered us into the back, away from the other staring parents looking on wide-eyed in the waiting room. The remedy for his reaction consisted of three doses of a heavy-duty antihistamine. Thankfully, despite the physical appearance and obvious tremendous external swelling, his throat had remained open, he had not experienced an anaphylactic reaction.

Forty-five minutes later, we were back in the car with a prescription for an EpiPen™, a pre-loaded, single-dose shot of epinephrine, intended to halt and reverse anaphylactic shock. The pediatrician warned me that allergic reactions such as Luke experienced are unpredictable. Additional exposure to nuts could trigger a more severe reaction next time. My son had been fortunate. Standing there sweaty and shaking at the pharmacy counter, I whipped out my credit card to pay for the pricey prescription without any hesitation. I'd just watched my son inflate like a balloon. He could have died. In that moment, the cost of the little life-saving device was irrelevant. I'd have paid any price for the assurance that if that happened again I could do something to save my child.

Luke is sixteen years old now, and still just as allergic not only to peanuts, but all nuts. He has suffered through allergy testing at three different points in his young life, at various ages, to see if by chance he had outgrown the allergy. When he was thirteen, we came away from the last visit to the allergist with a disappointing but firm diagnosis: he will always be allergic to nuts. We also came away that afternoon with a refill prescription for his EpiPen™.

Before I could get to the pharmacy, my phone rang,

"Mrs. Camealy?"

"Yes?"

I sensed by his hesitation that pharmacist was calling with bad news. His pauses were heavy. I could feel him bracing himself for my reaction.

"The deductible for the Epipen™ prescription we are filling for your son has gone up. It is higher than you might be expecting."

"What does that mean? How much is it?" I held my breath as he quoted me the price for the life-saving device.

"Would you still like me to fill the prescription for you?"

My shoulders sagged beneath my seatbelt. I hesitated. For sixteen years we have bought these life-saving pens, and never had to use the device once. With three other children, numerous other medical bills, ongoing orthodontia expenses, ophthalmology exams and potential vision therapy, not to mention dance lessons, horseback riding tuition, and new clothes for summer all also on the table at that same moment, the cost seemed exorbitant for an item that in all likelihood would expire and be thrown out without ever being used.

The accumulation of needs skewed my perspective. Did we really need it? We take care to diligently keep my son away from nuts. Maybe we could simply take extra precautions. I mean, I'm not a first-time mom any longer. I wrestled these thoughts in the brief seconds while the pharmacist waited on the line for my answer. For a fleeting moment, our diligent effort and the weight of the other expenses nearly fooled me into believing that the pen is unnecessary, that we could be careful enough, in our own effort—that if we just follow the safety guidelines, we could forgo the costly device. As I considered our safety measures, I fought the temptation to embrace a false sense of security and assurance based on our practices and experience. Dumbstruck from sticker shock, I momentarily questioned the value of the device. Is it worth it? With the phone pressed to my ear, I experience a sudden moment of clarity. Wait - we are talking about my boy's life. My love for my son turns the question inside out. I'm no longer asking is it worth it? The question becomes is he worth it?

"Yes, I want it." I respond. "I'm on my way now."

No matter the cost.

What Must I Do?

I'll bet the rich young man never forgot the day he approached Jesus with the question: "What must I do to inherit eternal life?" (Mark 10:17). Essentially, the man is asking How much does eternity cost? How can I experience authentic, abundant eternal friendship with you God? What do I lack? What does it take to be part of your Kingdom? Jesus responds, pointing out the necessity of obeying several of the commandments, to which the young man eagerly replies that he has already done so all of his life:

"Teacher, all these I have kept from my youth," he responds enthusiastically (Mark 10:20).

I imagine his momentary relief, as the young man puffs his chest a little proudly, overjoyed that he has checked those boxes. But before he has a chance to enjoy this response, Jesus continues, "You lack one thing: go, sell all that you have and give to the poor, and you will have treasure in heaven; and come, follow me" (Mark 10:21).

Close your eyes for a minute and put yourself in his sandals. Can you imagine what the young man must have been feeling, or what he must have been thinking? *Ok, no murder, no stealing, I've kept the laws with great effort. No adultery, I've honored my father and mother—I've been doing this since I was just a child. Now, wait—what? Sell everything? Lord, do you have any idea how long, how hard I have worked to get to this place? How much I've sacrificed to become the man I am today?*

Like my pharmacist on the other end of the line, Jesus stands before the man asking, "This is what it costs. Do you want it?" Actually, the question wasn't "Do you want it?" but "Do you want Me?"

"For where your treasure is, there your heart will be also."

Matthew 6:21

Jesus wasn't telling the man that only those who lack money can be with Him; what He was getting at was the greed that had infected the young man's heart. When Jesus said, "Take care, and be on your guard against all covetousness, for one's life does not consist in the abundance of his possessions (Luke 12:15)," He was speaking about the sin of greed.

When we're standing in the pews on Sunday mornings, are our hearts fully present or are they elsewhere? We hold our hymnals and watch the big screens and our lips move as the words tumble out, but are we aware of what we are saying? Are the hymns we sing the prayers and worship they are intended to be, or are they an automatic response to our environment, a box we are checking?

We sing, "I surrender all" but do we? Or do we surrender some, what we hope to be just enough. We know others who enjoy what seems to be an intimate friendship and vibrant fellowship with God. How does that happen? Jesus tells the rich young man to trade his tangible, hard-earned earthly wealth for "treasure in heaven"—a treasure the man cannot see or access or use as currency in any way here on earth. Jesus' entire ministry was always ever about transforming hearts, not the social status of His followers. When He called the disciples, they deliberately abandoned their jobs, thereby abandoning any promise of financial stability or social acceptability.

"While walking by the Sea of Galilee, he saw two brothers, Simon (who is called Peter) and Andrew his brother, casting a net into the sea, for they were fishermen. And he said to them, "Follow me, and I will make you fishers of men." Immediately they left their nets and followed him. And going on from there he saw two other brothers, James the son of Zebedee and John his brother, in the boat with Zebedee their father, mending their nets, and he called them. Immediately they left the boat and their father and followed him."

Matthew 4:18-22

When Jesus calls us, it comes at a cost. Jesus didn't come to make us comfortable. The gospel is not a "feel-good" message in the ways we are accustomed to. Those who know Jesus intimately will attest to the fact that transformation comes through sacrifice, surrender, refining and often, suffering. Jesus' disciples would learn this from the very beginning, and Jesus Himself would demonstrate this for us in His crucifixion. Intimacy with the Almighty is, as Charles Swindoll refers to it, "reserved for those whose hearts are completely His."[1]

Half-hearted

Who or what holds the affection of our hearts? When I look at my calendar, and where I devote the bulk of my time, what story does it tell about what has captured my affections? What about my bank account? My closet? My refrigerator and pantry? My home, and my relationships? Each of these things tell their own version of what holds my affinity. Funny how I prefaced each of them with the word "my," isn't it?

Do our hearts belong solely to God? What do our choices and commitments look like when held up for scrutiny in the light? Can we say without hesitation, that God reigns in every area of our daily coming and going? Do we submit our decisions and preferences to Him, and release the ones He requires us to abandon? What we refuse to surrender reveals the shape of our relationship with God. Are we not most often somewhat like the rich young ruler, disappointed with the impossibly high standards that God holds for us? What about the things He allows to be taken from us—how do we react when we're cornered into surrender, against our own desires and intentions?

Can we honestly say that we are living as Charles Swindoll says, as "completely His"? I cannot. Not all of the time, anyway.

I have, like the young ruler, accumulated for myself, things, a reputation. I have, by worldly standards, a measure of wealth that affords me certain comforts and pleasures unattainable to others outside of my socio-economic standing. These are God's gifts, to be sure. These are not things I deserve, nor can I truly lay any claim to them. But I often exercise a heavy measure of ownership over them, as if they were mined out of my own efforts and ability. The book of James reminds me that "Every good gift and every perfect gift is from above, coming down from the Father of lights with whom there is no variation or shadow due to change"

(James 1:17). I can become possessive about the things that God has given me by His grace.

A few years ago, when I lost a job that I loved, and that had come to me without me even filling out an application, I came face to face with my own struggle to accept a situation that did not unfold the way I'd wanted it to. How could God allow this, I'd thought then. He knows I need that income. This possessiveness causes me to balk at His holy demands for me to surrender back something He has shared with me for a season. When God asks me to surrender something, I struggle to say as Job did, "The LORD gave, and the LORD has taken away; blessed be the name of the LORD" (Job 1:21). Do I bless or resist Him?

So, how much does it cost? An intimate friendship and abundant fellowship with Jesus requires us to lay aside anything we hold dearer than Jesus Himself. It requires us to repeatedly surrender whatever it is that has captivated our hearts in that moment, every moment. The man wanted to know what it cost to enjoy this kind of enduring relationship with God, and Jesus' response was simple: sell everything. All of it. It wasn't the answer the young man was hoping for. It isn't the answer we are looking for either.

"Disheartened by the saying, he went away sorrowful, for he had great possessions."

Mark 10:22

Paying The Price

Questioning the value of a life-saving device for my child won't win me any mother-of-the-year awards. I cried on a friend's shoulder the day God reminded me of this story, and how I needed to share it with you. I resisted writing it for a couple of weeks asking God for a different example, something less ugly, less revealing about the shape of my own selfish heart. In the end, I surrendered to writing it, for two reasons: first, because God asked me to, and second, because God used it to once again, teach me about surrender.

Maybe you've never debated the cost of a medicine for one of your children, but chances are good that you've been tempted to skip making other necessary sacrifices at some point in your life. When confronted with a weighty decision, the question we ultimately want answered first is, *Is it worth it?* We want to know what God will do with our obedience. Our selfish tendencies don't lend themselves well to what parents often refer to as "first-time obedience." When we feel God tugging at something we're holding on to, rarely is our first reaction to eagerly set it on the altar and back away. More likely, we skirt the issue, hedge our bets and argue our case in hopes He will relent and let us keep our "stuff."

When God whispers the call to the altar into our hearts, we clench our fists tighter and fret over what it will mean to lay the thing down. We would do well to live as Corrie Ten Boom learned to—open handed, "Hold everything in your hands lightly, otherwise it hurts when God pries your fingers open." This is what it means to become a "living sacrifice" to always be ready to surrender whatever God asks of us. To live out the active, enduring service of obedience.

Deep down, that's what we want. We want to belong fully to God. We want to rest in the arms of the One who knows us intimately, and want to know Him in this way too. Thankfully, the Hound Of Heaven[2] doesn't give up so easily. In His passionate pursuit of us, He continues to woo us, offering us ample opportunity to draw near. I am reminded of this in my less-than-perfect parenting moments, and any other time when I am faced with letting go of something that doesn't really belong to me anyway.

The rich young ruler stood face to face with Jesus and still couldn't bring himself to surrender the one thing that stood between him and a real, lasting relationship with God. We might be tempted to shake our heads, but if we're honest, we do the same thing, daily. We debate the worth of surrender, or as Bonhoeffer referred to it, "The Cost Of Discipleship."[3]

The Look Of Love

As I read and re-read the story of the young ruler in Mark, I was struck by one little phrase that appears just before Jesus lays the full weight of the cost out. The scripture reads, "And Jesus, looking at him, loved him." Don't miss that. Jesus looked at the man, and loved him. Go on and underline that. We will need to remember this. Surrender is hard, and we will never get it perfectly right. When we struggle, when God calls us to the edge of the altar, when we suffer, one of the first things we tend to forget is how much God loves us. When God has something hard to share with us, we are assured that Jesus sees us and He loves us.

Our human condition tempts us to think that if God really loved us, He wouldn't allow us to walk through fire. But what Jesus demonstrated with His own crucifixion is that love like His comes at a price. Arms stretched wide on the cross, He paid it all, and like the hymn reminds us, "all to Him we owe."[4] Remembering that we are loved, that we are seen, is the grace that carries us to the edge of the altar. It's God's love that enables us to submit our temporary treasures back to Him. As created beings, we can remember that we (along with all that we have) ultimately belong to the Creator. We are not our own; we were "bought with a price" (1 Corinthians 6:20).

> All to Jesus I surrender,
> All to Him I freely give;
> I will ever love and trust Him,
> In His presence daily live.
> I surrender all,
> I surrender all.
> All to Thee, my blessed Savior,
> I surrender all.
> All to Jesus I surrender,
> Humbly at His feet I bow,
> Worldly pleasures all forsaken;
> Take me, Jesus, take me now.

Do we sing these lyrics with a truly surrendered heart?

Perhaps God has already put His finger on the thing He wants from you. Maybe the weight of your surrender has your own shoulders slumped in disappointment as you consider the cost of an intimate, lasting relationship with God. We imagine ourselves somehow capable of managing life around having to surrender our dreams, our health, our finances, our reputations, our jobs, our children, and other hopes we hold dear. We believe we can hold on to it with one hand while holding onto Jesus with the other. But what God wants from us, what He asks of us, is both hands around His neck. Our whole heart fully devoted to Him.

"Anyone whose determined purpose is to become more deeply and intimately acquainted with Him cannot retain the rights to his own position or place...or be anxiously preoccupied with working out the details of his own life. There must be complete and unqualified reliance on the living Lord. In other words, one must develop the discipline of surrender."[5]

God, so often we find ourselves feeling the same surprise and sadness that this young man felt when he came to understand the "cost of discipleship." We can't really fathom the price You willingly paid for our lives, and yet we know that this is what it takes—a total surrender, even unto death. We know that everything is Yours, and that though we may agonize over relinquishing our treasures, You are looking on us with love and mercy in your eyes. You know how hard it is, and You know how beautiful the discipline of surrender is—even when it hurts like hell. God, the only way we can learn it is if You help us. Show us that by Your strength, and the indwelling of Your Spirit, we can embrace the high price of Your saving grace. Fashion our hearts to want You most of all.
In Jesus' name, Amen.

3

Refiner's fire

My heart's one desire
Is to be holy

Brian Doerksen, "Refiner's Fire"

When I was a teenager, young in my faith and naïve to the cost of discipleship, we used to sing this song at church called "Refiner's Fire." With eyes closed and hands raised, I'd sing the words, "ready to do your will". I loved the lyrics to that song, and being inexperienced in my walking with Jesus, I thought it was exactly what I wanted—to do His will. But I had yet to experience the burn of the "refiner's fire." I had no idea. Do any of us?

But we've all done this. We gather weekly in the pews of our local church, we sing our favorite worship songs and hymns. We drive along in our cars singing the words to familiar, favorite pop-Christian tunes playing on the radio. But our lips betray us.

I mean, who in their right mind sings, "Oh let this be, where I die. My Lord with thee, crucified,"[1] and means it?

Lighting a Match

It's 2008. I've just completed a hand-me-down Bible study a friend gave me, and prayed the riskiest prayer I've ever prayed: *Make me more like you, God.* I was restless and knew something was "off" in my spirit. I didn't mean I wanted to be god-like. I was asking to be re-made in Christ's image; I wanted to be transformed. I wanted to "walk the walk."

> Whoever says he abides in him ought to walk in the same way in which he walked.
>
> 1 John 2:6

In those restless moments, when I whispered this prayer, before sweeping my preschooler and toddler's breakfast remnants into the garbage, I genuinely wanted it.

I did not know what I was asking for. I forgot that before life, death is required.

> Unless a grain of wheat falls into the earth and dies, it remains alone; but if it dies, it bears much fruit.
>
> John 12:24

When I prayed that prayer, I didn't know that I'd struck a match. I had no imagination for how God might choose to answer such a bold ask. I'm not sure I even believed that He would.

Farmers and land management experts commonly practice something called "prescribed burns." They are exactly what they sound like—intentional fires set on a designated parcel of land for the betterment of the natural plant and animal environments. Sometimes, these fires are set to restore what has been damaged, and other times, these fires are set to remove pests or disease. As one can easily imagine, initially these burns come at a cost. In the immediate aftermath, what remains of the scorched earth looks like a wasteland. Once, while in Florida, I drove past an entire pine forest blackened and burned-out. Gone were the typical saw palmettos and wiregrass tucked beneath the boughs of the pines. For miles, nearly nothing remained but ashen stumps. Everything, once thriving, now reduced to ash.

It takes years for a burned-out forest to thrive again. It seems so harsh. I've wondered if there was another way to achieve the same outcome, without the burning. I've wondered how anything good can really be born out of such a loss. But as it turns out, some plants actually require the fire. In fact, without the fire, some plants are at risk of extinction. The longleaf pine is such a specimen. "Its life cycle begins when fire prepares the soil for a pine seed to germinate by clearing the ground and turning leaves, dropped pine needles and sticks into fertilizer. For years a young seedling looks like a fuzzy pipe cleaner, its bud protected by tight needles while it grows a deep taproot. A second fire frees the bud and a tree quickly shoots high into the sky, above the fire line. Fire literally stimulates the next generation of this fabulous tree."[2]

Healing and restoration come at a cost. This is true in nature, and it's true in people too. It's possible to have "an initial encounter with Jesus that doesn't lead to a life abiding with Jesus."[3] Left to our own devices, without the actual touch of God on our lives, we are at risk for what Mark Buchannan calls, "a conversion without regeneration."[4] We pray for redemption but we don't want it to hurt. We pray for God to make us more loving, or more kind, or more willing to abide by His word. But we fail to understand what it is we are asking for. We have no idea.

Here's the truth. We are always praying from a place of ignorance, since we do not know what to pray for, or as we should (Romans 8:26). This is not an insult. This is a result of being finite, limited, and distinctly human. God's ability and willingness to answer our naïve prayers is not dependent on whether or not we understand what it is we are asking for. God answers our prayers according to His good, perfect and loving nature. God knows infinitely more than we do, what we actually need, and how best to meet those needs. However imperfect my prayer, in that moment I meant it with my whole, foolish, naive heart. I wanted to be changed.

To this day, I can't get the image of those blackened fields and forests out of my mind. In our ignorance we don't count the cost. Some of us are terrible at math. We don't understand God's economy—we don't know God's arithmetic. We forget that though God often begins by way of subtraction—somehow, inexplicably, Kingdom economics always, confoundingly, leads to abundance. But let's be clear, we're not a hair's-breadth or a Prayer of Jabez[5] away from material abundance—this is no faith-prosperity equation. The abundance that comes by way of God's arithmetic is of a spiritual nature. God's abundance, to an un-surrendered heart, can look very much like an ashen forest.

When God strips our lives of the chaff in a manner that looks and feels like a personal "prescribed burn," what looks and feels like a negative is the beginning of something else entirely. This is foundation work. This is soil being prepared for new planting, for new growth. He expands our narrow places in ways that don't always look like expansion. In the same way that a thick, lush forest that appears to be thriving can be a hostile place for nearly-extinct species to get a foothold, it's entirely true that we can gain the whole world but lose our souls for clinging too tightly to the things we are afraid to see consumed by holy fire. Things aren't always what they appear to be. We can be physically or financially viable while our souls remain vacant—empty of purpose and true fulfillment.

It's entirely possible for us to lose ourselves trying to save our own lives. The upside-down Kingdom of God is always reminding us that becoming less full of ourselves leaves more room in our hearts for God to fill us with Himself.

Out Of A Stump, A Shoot

The prophet Isaiah sees a host of angels and hears the voice of the Lord, regarding the Israelites who have polluted the forests of their lives with idolatry, disobedience and disdain for the things of God. The Lord speaks a painful message to him—their redemption will come at a cost. Isaiah will carry a message from God, but the people will not listen. He will preach and be ignored until seemingly nothing remains.

Until cities lie waste without inhabitant, and houses without people, and the land is a desolate waste, and the Lord removes people far away, and the forsaken places are many in the midst of the land. And though a tenth remain in it, it will be burned again, like a terebinth or an oak, whose stump remains when it is felled. "The holy seed is its stump.

Isaiah 6:12-13

This burn had a purpose. From the ash of a despondent, disobedient nation would rise the Savior of the world. The holy seed a stump.

The Meltdown

Real-life transformation is neither pretty nor painless. I witnessed this myself the summer my children and I trapped 3 caterpillars in a jar with the hopes of observing their transformation. We stocked their jar with their favorite plants—the same carrot leaves we'd found them nibbling on in the garden. We provided a few drops of water and two small bits of twig arranged at an angle on which they could attach their cocoons. For a few days, the caterpillars busily ate and excreted with regularity. We *ooh-ed and aah-ed* at their quiet, steady activity, until one day without warning, we awoke to three dangling cocoons. I greeted this new development with wonder and disappointment. I'd hoped to observe the process of their entombment, but instead they'd shrouded themselves while we slept. I wondered how many of life's other mysteries are we asleep to?

Now our interaction with the caterpillars changed. We no longer fed them. We walked past the jars glancing at them, but no longer studying them. We'd stop to watch from time to time, but there was little to see. The mystery remained hidden right in front of eyes. Their paper-thin cocoon managed to conceal a great deal of wonder unfolding. But, every now and then, while we sat around the table situated in front of the plant window where we kept their jar, a wild wriggling would catch the corner of our eyes. In these moments, we would turn to see the cocoon shaking with frightening ferocity—back and forth. Some moments, the wriggling grew so intense, I worried that the cocoon might break free from the branch on which it hung. We speculated about what was happening during this spastic, hidden dance.

Simple as I am, I never imagined that the goings-on of transformation might be painful. Before I knew better, I imagined that the wings were somehow added to the existing caterpillar, who underwent a few additional changes, to emerge as this new, winged creature. I didn't know that becoming a butterfly came by way of subtraction.

Inside the cocoon, every piece of her old body liquified into a soup of her own proteins.[6]

Sometimes, this is how God answers our prayers for transformation. Rather than gaining the "wings" we desire, our lives are often reduced to something utterly unrecognizable. More often than not, the holy transformation of our souls means that we will be reduced to ash, to soup—to what feels like nothing. But it's not for nothing. God is no masochist. Remember the stump?

The problem is, with our lives in ashes, when we are soup, we don't remember that the holy seed is a stump. We forget that unless a grain of wheat falls into the earth and dies, it remains alone; but if it dies, it bears much fruit (John 12:24). Distracted and disabled by what looks and feels like destruction, we are tempted to take it personally. We cry It's my life! Of course it's personal. Except our life isn't ours, not entirely.

What's Mine Isn't Really Mine

Years ago, I had the strangest dream. In it, a man stood beside a boiling cauldron with what looked like a pitchfork in his hand, periodically poking it into a rolling boil. From time to time, large pieces of meat bobbed up to the surface. He examined them momentarily, then prodded them back down into the boil. Like a shepherd, he tended this deceased herd—patiently, persistently. In my dream I only saw him from behind. He never turned to look at me. He was focused on his work. I watched the steam rise in his face, but he remained undistracted. I watched with an inexplicable sense of knowing what I was witnessing in the dream was important. I could not look away. It was a burning-bush kind of moment. I didn't move. I didn't speak. There was nothing to hear. It was a silent film. It was a dream—I knew when I woke that it was a vision. The morning after this dream encounter with the shepherd of the dead herd, I wrote every detail down in my journal. I didn't know what it meant, but I knew without explanation that it was important. I carried this dream, this vision, for seven years before I came to understand.

The Old Testament bulges with stories about sacrifice. We can't turn more than a few pages without encountering a story that involves images of death, offering, worship (the right and the wrong kind), fire and purification. Altars are everywhere. In 2008, when I dreamt of this man standing focused over an enormous pot, I knew that the image was biblical, but I didn't understand what was happening, nor the significance of the pot, the fork, the meat. But this vision seared itself to me like a brand making a near-daily appearance in my thoughts. All these years later, I can still see it clearly. Unsure of the significance of it, I prayed for a revelation. Praying is a form of surrender. I could only wait for God's timing.

God may seem slow, but He is never late. In 2014, seven years after this dream, while reading my assigned scriptures for that day, I stumbled across a passage that rocked me in my seat.

Now the sons of Eli were worthless men. They did not know the Lord. The custom of the priests with the people was that when any man offered sacrifice, the *priest's servant would come, while the meat was boiling, with a three-pronged fork in his hand, and he would thrust it into the pan or kettle or cauldron or pot.* All that the fork brought up the priest would take for himself. This is what they did at Shiloh to all the Israelites who came there. Moreover, before the fat was burned, the priest's servant would come and say to the man who was sacrificing, "Give meat for the priest to roast, for he will not accept boiled meat from you but only raw." And if the man said to him, "Let them burn the fat first, and then take as much as you wish," he would say, "No, you must give it now, and if not, I will take it by force." Thus the sin of the young men was very great in the sight of the Lord, for the men treated the offering of the Lord with contempt.

1 Samuel 2:12-17, *emphasis added.*

As I read it, the hairs on my arms stood at attention. The

vision from that night rolled in slow motion, like a filmstrip behind my eyes. This passage was about offering. It was about sacrifice. And it was about thieving from God.

Eli, a priest in Israel, had two sons who had no scruples. These two heathens made a habit of demanding the choice cuts of the God-ordained sacrificial meat for themselves. If the people wouldn't give it to them willingly, they'd take it by force.

Imagine that you bake a birthday cake for your child and as soon as it's finished and decorated, the neighbor kid busts into your kitchen, demanding a huge piece of cake. When you tell him that it is not his cake, he slices into it anyway, and hauls off the biggest piece for himself. The fact that this cake is designated for your child is no deterrent to this little tyrant. He wants what he wants, and so he takes it, holding you at knife-point if necessary. This is an imperfect analogy, but this is essentially what Eli's punk sons were doing. Except this was way more serious than taking a piece of cake from a neighbor. They weren't only stealing from their fellow Israelites—they were stealing directly from the Lord.

What kind of person would do that?

Me.

You.

We do that.

One of the most oft repeated passages of God's word, well known to the Israelites at this time, is called the *Shema*. This prayer summarizes, in a few potent lines, how God is to be regarded by His people. Deuteronomy 6:5 gives us this command: "You shall love the Lord your God with all of your heart and with all of your soul and with all your might."

Jesus Himself echoes this in the New Testament.

"The most important is, 'Hear, O Israel: The Lord our God, the Lord is one. And you shall love the Lord your God with all your heart and with all your soul and with all your mind and with all your strength.'"

Mark 12:28

Surely none of us could read the passage from Samuel about Eli's sons, and condone their behavior. Their sin is obvious, flagrant even. But how many of us would be willing to admit that we can see ourselves in the place of Eli's sons, swiping the choice cuts of an offering for ourselves? Because Jesus went to the cross for the sins of the world—for our sins (1 John 2:2), His substitutionary death absolved the practice of animal offerings to absolve human sin (Hebrews 10:1-14). In repentance we don't come to Christ with a dove or a lamb, we come with only our hearts. The sacrifice God asks of those who claim Christ is only this: a heart wholly committed to loving God. That's it. That's everything. That is the first and greatest commandment.

So, what does this story of a couple of wicked men have to do with us now? This is the question I asked of God: "What's this got to do with me?" In the weeks that followed my question, God revealed various corners of my life that I'd held back from submitting to Him. Everything from my personal principles, to my political ideals, to pet sins and old wounds I didn't want Him to touch. If I say that I love God with all of my heart, then how I vote is God's business. "Separation of church and state" may be an American ideology, but it's not a real thing in God's economy. We can't rightly hold a political stance on issues that goes in direct opposition to God's Word. If I say that I am surrendered to His Lordship, then those sins I take great pains to justify (gossip, idolatry, jealousy, self-righteousness—just to name a few) need to be confessed and repented of daily. If God is asking for my whole heart, then those wounds I've carried hidden, the ones I've grown comfortable with, must not be withheld from His healing touch— no matter how painful the process may be. We cannot love God with all of our hearts when our hearts are divided. God's desire for us is to be whole and healed, and we can only be whole, healed people when we are wholly His.

For months, one-by-one, God systematically peeled back layers of the things and parts of myself that I'd yet to surrender fully to Him. I'd been afraid of the burn. Afraid of becoming soup. I mistakenly believed that it was *my* life. Romans 12:1 says, "Present your bodies as a living sacrifice, holy and acceptable to God, which is your spiritual worship." If this is the call on the life of a believer, then that means that every time I deny a piece of my life for the Lord's purposes, I am laying claim to something that doesn't ultimately belong to me. In essence, I am saying to the Creator of the Universe—*I don't care that You made me, I own this part of my life and You can't touch it.* I am, in a way, stealing from God.

As created beings, we don't belong to ourselves—no matter how much society tells us otherwise. If we declare that we love Jesus with our lips, then our lives must be transformed in such a way as to reflect what we profess. We have been bought with a price (1 Corinthians 6:20). We are not self-made. God asks for no less than our entire heart and yet we divide it up among our many loves, offering God whatever, if anything, is left, while holding back the places we are most afraid of losing.

Some of us are hungry for better, but we're scared to receive it. We imagine that if we hold back the pieces of our lives that we treasure most, that we can get by giving God the leftovers. There's an old word for this. We don't like it, it's not popular or nuanced enough for our current sensibilities, but it's called idolatry. Those things we refuse to release, those pieces of our lives that we are most afraid of seeing consumed by the Refiner's fire are idols to us. We may not understand God's reasons or His methods, but understanding isn't a requirement for reverence or obedience. God tells us plainly that in our humanness, we are incapable of understanding His ways.

> For my thoughts are not your thoughts, neither are your ways my ways, declares the Lord.For as the heavens are higher than the earth, so are my ways higher than your ways and my thoughts than your thoughts.
>
> Isaiah 55:8-9

This is where faith becomes paramount. This is also where many of us get hung up in our attempts to surrender to God's purposes and plans. We lay claim to our lives. We demand an explanation. We make our ability to understand God's purposes a prerequisite for our surrender. This is where our fear and our naïveté show up, clouding our vision, causing us to forget Isaiah's stump. Our misplaced ownership of our lives places us at risk for missing the gift of the burned-out forest—new life. Transformed life. Abundance.

> There shall come forth a shoot from the stump of Jesse, and a branch from his roots shall bear fruit... In that day the root of

Jesse, who shall stand as a signal for the peoples—of him shall the nations inquire, and his resting place shall be glorious.

Isaiah 11:1, 10

Purpose In The Pain

The caterpillars-turned-butterflies emerged seemingly overnight. We awoke one morning to find them winged, wet and still, clinging to their twigs. We gathered our jar and my camera and took them out to the garden for their big release. We sat for a while observing their slow movements, noting the detail and magnificence of their brilliant color and markings. They were completely different than before. As I watched them I realized something. For the first part of their lives, those critters had only ever seen life from ground level, scrimping and crawling along on their bellies. Before, they were mostly consumers, munching their way through the garden. Now they would see new things from a different perspective. Now, instead of simply consuming plants, they would be helping plants to reproduce. Life coming from death.

If we're willing to draw near to God, we're unlikely to escape the pain of transformation. I wish it wasn't so hard. Something, maybe even what feels like everything, will be lost in the Refiner's fire. But this is not the loss that it appears to be. There's purpose in the pain. God's love for us burns so pure, that when we stand close enough to Him, we will be altered by the heat of His Holiness.

"Holiness means something more than the sweeping away of the old leaves of sin: it means the life of Jesus developed in us."[7]

This is where new life begins. Swaddled in the cocoon of His love, we become something more than we imagined. No longer conformed to the world, we grow in the likeness of Jesus.

God, how difficult it is to pray "Thy will be done" and mean it. We are creatures of comfort, prone to taking the easiest way around the hardest things, even if it means we will lose out on some other good thing. Even if it means forsaking intimacy with You. God You know how the heartbreak of surrender distorts our perspective and in the heat of the moment, blinds us to Your goodness. We need Your eyes to see through the smoke. We need Your heart to persevere when the ground beneath us becomes unrecognizable. Jesus, hold our hands as we walk through the ashes. Give us the courage to surrender our whole selves to You. Everything is Yours. Sift us, God, bring to mind those things we've failed to see as Yours, and help us to toss them into the fire of Your love, that their hold on our hearts would be broken forever, and that in their place we would find new life in communion with You.
In Jesus' name, Amen.

4

I Am The Israelites

Take the very hardest thing in your life—the place of difficulty, outward or inward, and expect God to triumph gloriously in that very spot. Just there, He can bring your soul into blossom!

Lilias Trotter

We started packing on Christmas Day. The joy of our traditional Christmas breakfast and opening of gifts was tempered by the weight of the work that awaited us. Sitting surrounded by wrapping paper on the floor, I'd opened a gift—a large glass pineapple candle. I started to pull it all the way out of the box but stopped when I realized that swaddled in bubble wrap, it was half-packed already. So I left it as it was—one less thing, out of some hundred-thousand things, that I wouldn't need to pack for our impending move. While the kids continued to open their gifts, I sipped my coffee, quietly counting the additional items that I'd now need to find boxes for.

The move was our idea, but also it was an answer to prayer. One day while talking about the growth of our family, and with a burgeoning sense that we were being nudged towards practicing more hospitality towards friends and neighbors, my husband and I agreed that we both felt like it was time. Twelve years earlier, when we first moved in, we had one child and a small dog. Now we had four children. The walls felt as if they'd shrunk. We were living on top of each other.

When the appraisal came back, we took it as a sign. This was the heavenly yes we'd "beg-prayed" for—you know those prayers of desperation you pray on repeat because you feel to move without a CLEAR sign might bring calamity upon your head? —that's how we prayed over this move. These are the prayers motivated by fear. We pray this way most often, when we are afraid that God won't answer, that God is going to ask us to do something hard or scary—or worse, that He isn't even listening. Begging-prayers are how many of us approach the altar of surrender, it's how we respond when we catch a whiff of what smells like the wilderness.

Months earlier, as if in subconscious anticipation of this season, we'd begun the "great purge," ruthlessly tossing out things tucked away in closets and in the basement, untouched for the duration of our life in that space. In those days, I made bi-weekly trips to the thrift store to drop off donations, and purchased those large, black trash bags the way people buy milk or bread. In the relief of cleaning out, I did not anticipate the fear that seized my heart. A steady, unnerving flutter began in my chest.

Somewhere in the middle of the melee of packing and preparing the house for showings, what had seemed so solid a decision only a few days earlier now felt foolish. I second-guessed everything. It was January, after all. In Ohio. Nobody buys houses when there's snow on the ground, I reasoned. People move when the weather's warm. They don't move in the dead of winter. This whole idea suddenly seemed insane. What were we thinking?

Doubt.

Fear.

Distrust.

Cleaning out became my go-to distraction for the mounting angst I felt over the innumerable what-if scenarios rattling around in my head.

What if we can't sell this house?
What if we can't get enough money in the sale?
What if we can't find a new house?
What if something comes back on the house inspection that holds this whole thing up?
What if people hate the tiny kitchen?—I know they're going to hate this tiny kitchen. *I* hate this tiny kitchen.
What if we can't get financing?
What if we move and regret it?
What if, what if, what if—

I hadn't realized until the process began that in accepting what felt like God's invitation to move, we walked straight into what felt like the wilderness—a season of doubt, fear, and distrust.

Historically, wilderness seasons are places of great spiritual transformation. But most of us don't choose them. Our struggle to surrender is a lot like this. We know it's the right thing to do, but we don't often come to it willingly. We've got good reasons why we're better off holding on to our lives. We are professional rationalizationists. This is our heritage, dating all the way back to the Israelites. Aren't we born into the same heart-condition as people who, when plucked mercifully from the clutches of slavery, looked back at their seasons of oppression with deluded fondness? When God is moving us towards new places of freedom, don't we fret in our discomfort, and paint false, rose-colored histories of "the good ol' days"?

When Pharaoh drew near, the people of Israel lifted up their eyes, and behold, the Egyptians were marching after them, and they feared greatly. And the people of Israel cried out to the Lord. They said to Moses, "Is it because there are no graves in Egypt that you have taken us away to die in the wilderness? What have you done to us in bringing us out of Egypt? Is not this what we said to you in Egypt: 'Leave us alone that we may serve the Egyptians'? For it would have been better for us to serve the

Egyptians than to die in the wilderness."

Exodus 14:10-12

They set out from Elim, and all the congregation of the people of Israel came to the wilderness of Sin, which is between Elim and Sinai, on the fifteenth day of the second month after they had departed from the land of Egypt. And the whole congregation of the people of Israel grumbled against Moses and Aaron in the wilderness, and the people of Israel said to them, "Would that we had died by the hand of the Lord in the land of Egypt, when we sat by the meat pots and ate bread to the full, for you have brought us out into this wilderness to kill this whole assembly with hunger."

Exodus 16:1-3

There's truth, And There's Truth

We are a people made to tell stories. And we can tell some whoppers. We are masters at revisionist history. Every day, we are telling ourselves a story about who we are, who God is, and what it looks like in any given moment to live this current version of our story. But how we remember our history—not only our immediate history but our ancestral history as God's people, inevitably shapes the stories we tell ourselves and others. We have a decidedly short memory in light of eternity. Our penchant for forgetting the unwavering goodness of God leaves us wrestling with Him when the invitation at hand is to let go and receive.

The stories we tell ourselves about ourselves matter, but even more important are the stories we tell ourselves about God. God's specific location in our unfolding story impacts not only whether or not we receive God, but also *how* we receive Him. It's entirely possible to know about God without knowing Him at all. Our proximity to God becomes vividly clear when the barren landscape of wilderness seasons invite us into unfamiliar territory. Stripped of our usual comforts and distractions, our imaginations work to make sense of these new, usually unwelcome, surroundings.

Whether we walked willingly into the wilderness, or were led up there by the Spirit (Matthew 4:1) matters less than the narrative we tell ourselves about why we are there in the first place, and where we imagine God is in our wandering.

Tozer wrote that "what comes into our minds when we think about God is the most important thing about us."[1] C.S. Lewis argued that "How God thinks of us is not only more important, but infinitely more important. Indeed, how we think of Him is of no importance except in so far as it is related to how He thinks of us."[2]

How we think of God matters, because whatever character we ascribe to Him, will shape our willingness to worship Him, our willingness to surrender to Him. And at the same time, God's thoughts about us bear infinite worth because His thoughts are rooted in Himself, as our perfect Creator. We are his offspring (Acts 17:28).

What if, rather than dreading them as seasons of oppression, we considered wilderness seasons as an opportunity to grow deeper in our faith while discovering Emmanuel—the God who is with us always?

How we frame our current situation shapes how we respond to it. Our culture embraces the concept that truth is fluid, that we each get to have our own truth. But little *t* truth is not the same as big *T* Truth. Sure, we have our own unique experiences that cause something to be true for us as individuals, but that *t*ruth does not supersede the *T*ruth that is woven into all of creation by the God who made the heavens and the earth, the sea and everything in them (Psalm 146:6).

The distinction here between *t*ruth and *T*ruth is always pivotal, but perhaps most especially so when we find ourselves thrust into a season of struggle and hardship. It's an easy mistake to confuse the *t*ruth of our personal experiences with the *T*ruth of what God is doing in the midst of our wrestling season. And as the Exodus account reveals, it's also a costly mistake.

Plunged into the wilderness by way of the Red Sea, the Israelites found themselves experiencing a life they no doubt only dreamed of. Released from the clutches of slavery, they found themselves closer to God than ever. But they were thirsty, and water is no easy resource to find in the desert. In their thirst, they grumbled against Moses (Exodus 15:24). By way of God's kindness, God turns bitter water sweet, reviving His people (Exodus 15:25). But it doesn't take long for a new complaint to arise—this time, they are hungry. In classic, revisionist history form, they recall the abundance of food that they had back in Egypt.

And the whole congregation of the people of Israel grumbled against Moses and Aaron in the wilderness, and the people of Israel said to them, "Would that we had died by the hand of the Lord in the land of Egypt, when we sat by the meat pots and ate bread to the full, for you have brought us out into this wilderness to kill this whole assembly with hunger."

Exodus 16:2-3

Did you catch that? The *truth* about the difficulty of their circumstances minimizes the *Truth* of what God is doing for them. In Chapter 15, they are singing the song of Moses, praising God for their salvation and rescue:

"Who is like you, O Lord, among the gods? Who is like you, majestic in holiness, awesome in glorious deeds, doing wonders? You stretched out your right hand; the earth swallowed them. "You have led in your steadfast love the people whom you have redeemed—

Exodus 15:11-13

And only a short while later, they have begun to tell themselves a different story. Now, God is not praised, but instead is painted as uncaring. Perhaps, with stomachs rumbling, they even imagine Him cruel. They go so far as to accuse Him of attempted murder.

"For you have brought us out into this wilderness to kill this whole assembly with hunger."

This is only a snapshot of a longer story that unfolds for forty years. The remainder of the book of Exodus offers numerous accounts similar to this, where the *truth* of circumstances supersedes the *Truth* of God's continual provision, presence, and protection. The most devastating hardship to befall the Israelites in the wilderness always came on the heels of trading their perception of *t*ruth for God's ultimate Truth.

Untethered from the Truth, we can convince ourselves of anything. Unmoored, we can convince ourselves that letting go of expectations and prescribed outcomes is dangerous—too risky to be embraced. Disconnection from Truth leads to disobedience. It leads to irreverence. Divorced from the Truth of who God is, we can come to believe that God's best intentions for us are not as kind as we've previously imagined. However true this may seem to us in our moments of struggle, historically this is false. Isaiah 43 is not a poem, it is a promise.

When you pass through the waters, I will be with you; and through the rivers, they shall not overwhelm you; when you walk through fire you shall not be burned, and the flame shall not consume you.

Isaiah 43:2

Afraid to Wander

As a military brat, I spent the first eighteen years of my life moving to a new state, every two years. Even as a youth, I knew the work of packing a house and preparing it for sale, but I forgot about how the depths of upheaval can overtake you when your house is in disarray and there are innumerable decisions that need to be made quickly. Our core values and beliefs are always rooted out under the strain of uncertainty and questioning. Wilderness seasons are a plunge into the refining fire. It makes little difference whether that season lasts a week or a few years. Our surrender-reflexes are tested, and our all-too-often flimsy faith crumbles under the weight of our fears when our usual comforts are disrupted. Like our ancestors who longed to return to slavery, we look over our shoulder at what was with distorted fondness because we are afraid:

Afraid of what we can't see
Afraid of what we can't control
Afraid of what might happen

> Afraid of what might not happen
> Afraid of what others will think
> Afraid of what we might lose
> Afraid we don't have enough (money, materials, help, ability, etc)

Walking into a wilderness season more often than not feels like stumbling around in the dark. Barbara Brown Taylor noted that "from the earliest times, Christians have used 'darkness' as a synonym for sin, ignorance, spiritual blindness, and death." She notes a handful of serious problems created by embracing this narrative at face value, citing that "worst of all, it offers people of faith a giant closet in which they can stuff everything that threatens or frightens them without thinking too much about those things."[3]

But the refining fires of desert seasons burn away the chaff. In the desert, we are exposed for who we really are.

Trust

The mounting unknowns of our impending move left me irritable and restless. The fluttering in my chest grew more persistent. I worked my way through the house with razor-focus, painting, packing, cleaning. I distracted myself with coffee and regular trips to big box stores to collect flattened boxes and packing materials. As long as I kept working, I could half-drown out the anxiety of uncertainty. But running from fear is a poor coping mechanism. Fear is always faster. Plus, it never peters out. A couple of weeks later, I landed on the exam table at my doctor's office, wired to a heart monitor.

> "When we run from darkness, how much do we really know about what we are running from? If we turn away from darkness on principle, doing everything we can to avoid it because there simply is no telling what it contains, isn't there a chance that what we are running from is God?"[4]

Insert the word "wilderness" or "unknown" for darkness in this quote. We are talking about the same thing. I was afraid of the ways this move could unravel our lives. But what I was most afraid of, what I was running from, was God.

Fear causes us to second-guess both God and ourselves. Concerns about the innumerable what-if scenarios we conjure up in our minds, become like the tendrils of a weed that wind themselves around us and choke out our confidence in who we know God to be. We assume that seasons of uncertainty and difficulty must mean that we have taken a wrong turn—that we have slipped beyond the borders of God's will. Or worse, that God is "out to get us." But this idea is not supported anywhere in scripture. In fact, the Word tells us specifically that struggle and difficulty are both a promise, as well as part of our holy calling.

"In the world you will have tribulation. But take heart; I have overcome the world."

John 16:33

Beloved, do not be surprised at the fiery trial when it comes upon you to test you, as though something strange were happening to you. But rejoice insofar as you share Christ's sufferings, that you may also rejoice and be glad when his glory is revealed.

1 Peter 4:12-13

We are promised hardship, and we are promised God's presence in the midst of our suffering. The desert is a place of close companionship with the Holy One. In the two most significant desert stories in scripture, God is wildly near.

And the Lord went before them by day in a pillar of cloud to lead them along the way, and by night in a pillar of fire to give them light, that they might travel by day and by night. The pillar of cloud by day and the pillar of fire by night did not depart from before the people.

Exodus 13:21-22

Then Jesus was led up by the Spirit into the wilderness to be

tempted by the devil...Then the devil left him, and behold,
angels came and were ministering to him.

Matthew 4:1,11

A Diagnosis

In the middle of painting the walls and packing boxes, I wore a
Holter monitor for a couple of days. The heart palpitations that
had set in, almost as soon as we began house hunting, were not
a figment of my imagination. Every few minutes, what felt like
an internal butterfly would flutter its wings in the center of my
chest. Every flutter set me further on edge. Maybe I was dying.
Maybe this terrible season of obedience was in fact slowly killing
me. I was afraid to sleep. Afraid to travel too far from home.
Afraid to overexert myself lifting and hauling things from the
house. The only scenarios that played out in my mind were
negative.

As optimistic as I normally am, in my mind there could be
no positive explanation for what was happening. Surely, God
had brought me out into this wilderness to kill me.I resented
how weak I felt. I resorted to my old ways, attempting to hoist
myself up by my bootstraps. The voice in my head spoke harshly
to me, snarling things like, get it together and you're a real
mess! Trusting God didn't seem to be getting any easier. I
wondered if in the years since God had interrupted my
comfortable deceptions, if I'd learned anything at all about Him.
In my anxiety-riddled frame of mind, my posture towards
surrendering to the season we were in stiffened. With every
flutter, I was rewriting the story, laying the *truth* of my current
experience over the *Truth* of what I knew about God.

While God hadn't ordered us to move, we could not deny
that we both felt led towards making real room for hospitality
towards others. Our current home simply would not allow us to
embrace the vision God seemed to be sharing with us. The
necessary circumstances were aligning in such a way that
seemed, by all appearances, to be a holy ordinance. The doors
were opening. The pieces were falling into place. Like Gideon,
we are a people who need signs to know that we are hearing

correctly from God.

Show me a sign that it is you who speak with me.

Judges 6:17

By our interpretation, the signs were all there. In this way, moving felt like something we could not say *no* to. Nor did we want to. When the report finally came back from my doctor, I was relieved to know I wasn't dying. It turned out the flutter in my chest was caused by something far uglier than a butterfly. My diagnosis: *acute anxiety*. The prescription my doctor offered was a mix of practicing relaxation techniques and "no caffeine." I left the office relieved that I wasn't straddling this move with one foot in the grave. But no caffeine? —God was taking away my bitter water.

The Promise of His Presence

To my chagrin, January turned out to be the perfect month to list our house. Within thirty days of putting it on the market, we had a signed offer from a young couple. We'd said all along that the only people our home would appeal to was either a young couple or empty-nesters. These two were about to be married and needed a place to live. Our realtor told us that they had made offers on numerous other homes, but lost those contracts in bidding wars. Bidding wars in January? I felt God winking at me. Given their circumstances, negotiations went down easily.

During our search for a new home, we stumbled on a house in a neighborhood we hadn't even considered. For whatever reason, it had not been listed in any of the real estate MLS listings. It was brand new and we knew from the moment we walked into the great room flooded with the afternoon light, this was THE ONE.

But it wouldn't be that easy. It was out of our price range. We'd spend the next couple of weeks agonizing over our budget, and negotiating with the builder, beg-praying that somehow God would make a way.

What I didn't know then, but learned within days of moving in, was that our new-to-us next door neighbors had been praying fervently for whatever family would buy the house next to them. Their faith in God's provision played an integral role in us receiving the keys to our home. That they prayed so earnestly for us humbled me. The day my new neighbor stood in my entryway and shared this secret with me, I knew God was teaching me something.

What we lacked in trust, God provided through the unwavering faith of strangers. In this unseen way, God was with us in our wilderness. In every twist and turn of the situation, God passed through the rocks that we saw as obstacles to our dreams, revealing Himself in numerous ways.

The truth was that our struggle to trust God with our needs and desires did not obliterate His presence from our situation. In our grumbling and fear, God was working. God doesn't ask for a perfect surrender. But He does ask us to be willing. He invites us to come experience His presence in the midst of difficulty.

God is our refuge and strength, a very present help in trouble. Therefore we will not fear though the earth gives way, though the mountains be moved into the heart of the sea, though its waters roar and foam, though the mountains tremble at its swelling.

Psalm 46:1-3

I know how this sounds. Even while battling anxiety and the stress of packing, we still ended up in a house better than we dreamed of, and it's amazing, and we are so happy. It sounds like a fairy-tale, huh? What if we hadn't gotten the financing? Or if that young couple had actually hated our tiny kitchen and changed their minds during the final walk-through? What if we'd lost our bid against other buyers for this place?

Plenty of faith-filled Christians are living stories that don't end the way ours did. Checks don't always come in the mail. Medical intervention doesn't always work. Sometimes, the diagnosis is worse than acute anxiety. I don't understand these things. All I can do is be a witness to what God has done in my life, to what He's shown me. And while moving into that new house was wonderful, the bigger piece of the whole story was seeing (once again) that what feels like the dark is not dark to Him (Psalm 139).

God, our fears can seem insurmountable. We are afraid of so many things. But the wilderness was never meant to be a place of exile for us. In the desert You wooed Your people with Your constant presence and provision, even when it looked different than their expectations. And You're doing it still for us today. You are with us even now, in seasons of prosperity and devastation. You have not brought us to this moment to die, but rather to teach us what it means to really live in Your presence. You are always leading, if only we would open our hearts to Your kind guidance. Everything is Yours, God. Help us to receive You even now. Help us to remember that the dark we fear is not dark to You. Lead us through into Your Light. Give us hearts and minds of confident hope that in Your timing, and in Your way, all shall be made well.
In Jesus' name, amen.

5

Selah

Let that grace now like a fetter, bind my wandering heart to thee. Prone to wander, Lord I feel it, prone to leave the God I love. Here's my heart O take it seal it. Seal it for thy courts above.

Robert Robinson

Shrek. Okay, what image immediately comes to your mind? Maybe you immediately picture the lovable green ogre with Mike Myers's voice? That's fair. That used to be the first image that came to my mind when I heard it, until I read a certain news story about a sneaky sheep by the same name. Let me tell you briefly about Shrek, a merino sheep in New Zealand who managed to evade his shepherd for seven years by hiding out in a series of caves. When Shrek the sheep was finally discovered, he sported about sixty pounds of wool—enough to produce twenty men's suits.[1] The story goes that Shrek wasn't all that interested in being sheared, so he took to the hills as a means of avoiding the mandatory clipping he'd normally be subjected to. Sneaky, huh?

I've thought about this particular sheep for years since I first read about his high jinks in the caves of New Zealand. His story of taking to the hills and hiding out, rather than living shepherded and tended to by his owner, strikes me as both amusing and uncomfortably familiar. I see myself in Shrek, my own propensity towards sneaking away from my Shepherd. How many times have I wandered like a runaway sheep (Psalm 119:176)?

Of course, at least in part, Shrek's story resonates with me because of scripture's repeated references to God's people being like sheep. In the 10th chapter of the book of John, Jesus uses this metaphor to make His point,

"I am the good shepherd. The good shepherd lays his life down for the sheep."

John 10:11

A quick study on the nature of sheep leaves us tempted towards offense at God's pet name for His people. Referring to people as "sheep" has never implied a compliment. Calling someone by that name usually suggests their willingness to follow the crowd without a thought, regardless of whether or not their blind following will lead them into prosperity or destruction. Sheepish people lack self-confidence, and usually present an embarrassed face. Sheep are not often recognized for their high intelligence in the way that some animals are. Instead, sheep are ruled by a heightened flocking instinct. This strong, instinctual nature can be disastrous, as it was in 2006 when one fool sheep grazing a hillside in Turkey attempted to cross a wide ravine. Unable to accurately judge the gap, this wayward sheep inadvertently led 400 others to their death at the bottom of the ravine. The others followed him over the edge, purely out of instinct.[2] The point being that sheep need a shepherd. And while I prefer to think of myself as a little sharper of mind and more capable than these wooly beasts of the field, I have to confess I'm prone to wander and follow the herd. I do this even though I know how vulnerable that leaves me to harm, or the enemy that loves nothing more than to steal.

"The thief comes only to steal, kill and destroy. I came that they may have life and have it abundantly."

John 10:10

Worship As An Act of Surrender

We currently live in one of the most self-centered periods in history. With the advent of various social media platforms, we can now build our own cyber towers of Babel blasting out selfies and snapshots of our perfectly cropped lives to hundreds of thousands of people at a time. We have access to concrete data to measure our self-worth, our recognition. We have our own little glory-meter in our pocket able to update our ranking minute by minute.

We crave the power and glory due a king. But few of us carry the wisdom or humility necessary to wield it with honor and responsibility. Our fear of being forgotten twists our intentions, motivating us to work at making much of ourselves. Despising our smallness, we spend our lives climbing ladders of various heights at the expense of our families, our dignity, and our commitment to following Christ. We build false personas online, and even in our flesh-and-blood social circles, carefully sculpting what we want others to see and know about us. Our emotions rise and fall with the pulse of societal beats. We listen too easily to the voices of the many over the voice of the One.

I recently took an informal Facebook poll. I asked people to share about their struggles with identity. The responses all included our common struggle to understand who we are apart from our accomplishments and deficiencies. For so many of us, our identity is bound up in the opinions of others, and in our ability to perform (to our own standards and the standards of others). The poll simply showed me something I'm already aware of in my own life: we don't know who we are.

All we like sheep have gone astray; we have turned everyone to his own way; and the LORD has laid on Him, the iniquity of us all.

Isaiah 53:6

Our identity, or knowing who we are, is vitally important when we think about living a life of worship. That's because we are made to worship—which is not the same as being made to be worshipped (Isaiah 43:7). Having an inaccurate understanding of our identity confuses our worship. Remember how scripture starts? In the beginning God—

> God breathed creation into existence.
> God announced the stars.
> God made the waters team with fish and the
> skies fill with flocks of birds.'
> God set down on the earth, animals of all
> species and kinds.

God's glory filled the earth. God knelt down in the dirt, and sculpted a man—Adam, and breathed life into him, and then created woman out of him (Genesis 2:22).

We who are created beings have, since the first juicy bite of forbidden fruit, imagined in our fool-minds that we have transcended our Maker. Our deception, our self-inflation has warped our minds and hearts so out of shape, that rather than pursue intimacy with our Father in heaven, rather than stick by the Shepherd, we fall down at the feet of nearly anything else, including ourselves. We sell our souls for sex, drugs, power, success, fame, money, alcohol, health, and whatever other passionate pursuit that dogs us in our daily living. Forgetting who we are, who we were created to be, we have exchanged the truth about God for a lie and worshipped and served the creature rather than the Creator (Romans 1:25). When we are confused about who God is, we cannot know who we are. And we wander like sheep.

A Child Will Lead Us

When my youngest was barely two, she began the practice of bowing her face to the floor during bedtime prayers. The first time I watched her do it, I remember the goose bumps that immediately prickled the surface of my skin. She certainly didn't learn that posture from me. I had not yet learned true surrender and was in fact in a season of holy wrestling with God at that very same time. In those days, I still prayed with clenched fists and a stiff neck. But there she was, in her green footed pajamas, on her knees, bent at the waist, face to the floor, with her tiny arms out in front of her, her chubby toddler fingers laced together above her head. I remember staring at her in wild wonder mixed with deep conviction.

The winter I came face-to-face with my own actual human nature was a difficult one. Up until a come-to-Jesus encounter with the Lord in my closet one afternoon, I imagined myself to be far more capable and self-sufficient than I actually am. That season God asked me to let go of a long-held dream. I'd spent months praying about it, telling God how much it was ultimately His, and that I would let Him steward it. But when God made it clear He was asking me to release it, when the doors that had once been opened to me regarding this dream all slammed shut, when I knew God was asking me to surrender it back to Him, I would not relent. His request revealed the chasm between the prayers I'd prayed and my own actual willingness to let it go.

A fight ensued. With my spiritual heels dug in, I wrestled Him for it. I would not let it go. I believed it was mine, and that in my own strength and by might, I could steward it into fruition. I will say more about this season in the next chapter, but for now, you need to know that it was a knock-down, drag-out brawl with God, like Jacob and the angel (Genesis 32:22-31).

Pride is not easily killed. The voice inside of me sounded like the serpent in the garden, challenging the very word of God, encouraging me to elevate myself above my Creator. Like Eve, I gulped it down, greedily exchanging the truth for a lie. I was a sheep approaching the edge of a ravine I didn't have the sense to spot. With my feet dangerously close to the edge, God mercifully called me out of my sin. In that moment of conviction, it was as if I heard the footfalls of the Lord in my very own bedroom, as He called to me—*Where are you?* (Genesis 3:9) It wasn't an audible voice that I heard, but the sensation that struck me so sharply in my spirit it may as well have been. I heard His voice, and I knew Him.

> The sheep hear his voice, and he calls his own
> sheep by name and he leads them out.

John 10:3

On my face in my closet, with my hands outstretched in front of me, I poured out the contents of my heart before the Lord. In His love, God opened my eyes to the numerous ways I'd worshipped myself, the ways I'd refused to surrender to God. I'd hidden it well from the world, but thankfully God sees all things (Luke 8:17). What I discovered in those moments of repentance was the ways my wandering had hindered my willingness to let God all the way in.

We worship the object of our affections. The pride I took in my ability to accomplish tasks, achieve success and spin numerous plates at once had made me feel powerful. And without realizing it, I had become the object of my worship. I gave God lip-service when I felt like it, but my heart was not set on Him. Until that moment, I'd been unaware—clueless about how far I had wandered from the safety of my Shepherd. I'd grown a thick, matted coat of self-righteousness, while I'd lived tucked away in my hiding place. I imagined myself as better off and healthier than I was, while in reality, I was sicker than I knew.

God's reference to us as sheep is intended to be a simple analogy, giving us a picture of both our nature and God's. He takes the metaphor of us as His sheep further by calling Himself the Good Shepherd. In this, God gives us a clearer vision of His love and care for us. By calling us His sheep, God shows us exactly who we are—foolish, helpless and prone to wander, susceptible to predators and vulnerable to the elements, and He uses this analogy to demonstrate exactly who He is—caring, tender, and loving. Sheep learn to recognize the voice of their Shepherd (John 10:27).

We need the methodical, gentle and firm tending of the very God who made us and knows exactly how sheep-like we are. Learning the voice of the Shepherd allows us to find our home in the sanctuary of His pasture. Here with Him, Jesus says, we find eternal life, where no one will snatch us out of His hand (John 10: 28-30). Learning to abide with Christ re-orients our perception of who we are. In light of knowing how generously God tends His flock, how mercifully and patiently He cares for us, our hearts are moved to praise. Jesus literally saves our lives; how could we resist thanking Him for this kindness? How can we withhold gratitude for this display of love?

"It takes power, doesn't it, to thank the Father when everything in us protests? But we find in Him (not always in what happens to us) plenty of reason to thank Him and plenty of power."[3]

Prone to Wander

Who knows what it was that caused Shrek-the-sheep to take up residence in that cave for all of those years. It's somewhat miraculous that he survived so long on his own. Do sheep have opinions about shearing? Is that really what drove him into hiding? What about that intense flocking nature? Maybe God, in His infinite wisdom gave the world Shrek for the pure illustration that his story offers us, a present-day reminder of an age-old gospel story about God's purpose and plan for His people. It doesn't actually matter what Shrek's motivations were, but we can and should spend some time thinking about what motivates us to hide out from God.

Whatever Shrek's case may have been, his story reminds us that to some extent we're all prodigals fighting for independence, eager to risk it all to live life on our own terms despite the eternal danger that this puts us in. In our confusion or outright rejection of who God has created us to be, we are still worshipping something. It's impossible to worship God and run from Him at the same time. We can't wander off of a cliff when we're fixed in praise of the Shepherd who's leading us. Worshipping God out of obedience sets our hearts intently on the Lord. This kind of worship is not done as a gesture. No, this is a posture, the position of a sheep who is intent on following the Shepherd. Closely.

In his book *A Long Obedience In The Same Direction*, Eugene Peterson describes how worship transforms us: "Every time we worship, our minds are informed, our memories are refreshed with the judgements of God, we are familiarized with what God says, what he has decided, the ways he is working out our salvation."[4] In obedient worship, the Shepherd tunes our hearts to the sound of His voice. Denying our sheep-like tendencies signals that we're not ready to listen. It means we're off in a cave somewhere, doing it our own way.

Marked

One of the ways shepherds use to mark and identify their sheep is by tattooing. This method avoids damaging the wool or reducing the value of the animal at market. A few years ago, on a quiet morning in September, I climbed up into the black pleather chair at a local tattoo parlor and had forever imprinted on my forearm the line—*bind my wandering heart to thee*. That's a line from my favorite hymn, "Come Thou Fount of Every Blessing" by Robert Robinson. Having spent a great number of years in denial about my propensity to wander, this permanent mark on my arm is a constant reminder that if I do not remain bound to my Shepherd, if I offer my devotion at the altar of any other thing, I am living back in the cave, sheepishly confused as to just who I am and who God is.

But get this—the morning after I got my tattoo, I had this momentary thought: *Wait, I don't need this reminder—I never wander from God anymore.* I wish I could tell you I didn't have that thought, but I did. Yeah, can anybody say "p-r-i-d-e"? Ugh, the very fact that I felt so sure that I could manage this life without the temptation to wander off clearly reminded me how desperately I need to be bound to my Shepherd, the Good Shepherd who loves me and gave Himself for me. "If only we knew how we need God's grace and assistance, we would never lose sight of Him not even for a moment."[5]

> Oh, to grace how great a debtor
> Daily I'm constrained to be
> Let that goodness like a fetter
> Bind my wandering heart to Thee
> Prone to wander, Lord, I feel it
> Prone to leave the God I love
> Here's my heart, oh, take and seal it
> Seal it for Thy courts above

God, how often like sheep we have gone astray. The world is wide and wonderful and full of so many good and wonderful opportunities for us to explore. But it's also a wilderness, full of danger and dark caves we have no business hiding out in. And as much as we know in our heads the dangers of going off on our own, apart from You, the pull on our hearts is more than most of us can resist. And yet, wander as we will, there is no place we can hide from You—not really. You are with us everywhere, which, as much as we might think cramps our style, is a grace we cannot fully fathom. In Your loving kindness, with the gentle persistence of a Shepherd, You pursue us to the furthest caves and bring us back to You. Bind us to You, God. Tether our wayward hearts and our stubborn wills to Your Spirit, that we might learn the way of obedience. Help us to remember that everything is Yours—that we are Yours. Help us to understand that the greatest life we can ever live, is one nestled in the palms of your generous hands. Teach us what it means to be the sheep of Your pasture, and to abide with You, our Good Shepherd.
In Jesus' name, amen.

6

Ten Miles For Mani

Sometimes the things that hurt are worth the pain.

Jon Foreman

"Hey Krissie, it's Carrie."

"Hey Carrie! It's so good to hear from you!"

"So, I've been wanting to come and visit you for forever, and I had an idea—there's a race happening in September at a park near your house, and I wanted to know if you'd be willing to train with me to run it when I come visit?"

"A race—how many miles is it?" I held my breath in the pause.

I'd recently told Carrie how I'd been considering trying running as a method for losing the weight I'd gained during my last pregnancy, but I was still very new to the activity.

"Six miles."

Six miles seemed ambitious, but having become a participant in Compassion International's Child Advocacy program I'd been looking for a way to show my support, for both the child we sponsored as a family, and the greater ministry. I'd seen other people raise money through running races—how hard could it be?

We'd received a couple of photos of our sponsored child, Mani. I couldn't shake the image of his lean, dark body in clothes too small for him. Every letter we received from him told us a little more about his story. In one letter, he'd drawn a picture of the mud hut he shared with his family. He told us how his family used the extra funds we sent at Christmas to purchase beans. His family has to send someone with a water bottle or buckets for long distances to scoop dirty water from a river for their daily water needs. His family grows corn and beans, and this is their sustenance. If by running six miles I could help Mani, or another child like him, how could I possibly refuse?

Carrie and I mapped out a training program, finalized the details, and promised to hold each other accountable as we trained. We agreed to send text messages when we finished our daily runs and we'd track each other's progress through a fitness app we'd both downloaded to our phones. We had eight months to train; that seemed reasonable enough. With all of the logistical details nailed down, we were ready to get after it.

As soon as I hung up the phone, the gravity of my commitment settled on me. I had never run a race in my life. Also, I hated running.

In eighth grade, I played one season of soccer. All of my friends were on the team, and it was a good excuse to buy and wear the very-cool Umbro shorts that everyone else was wearing (I wish I were kidding about that last part). I'd joined that JV soccer team purely for the social aspect, not realizing how much running is required in soccer. Up and down the field. Back and forth. Over and over and over again, for what felt like a thousand hours in the blazing hot South Florida sun. I hated every minute of it. I played fullback because supposedly this position required the least amount of running. "Just hang out near the goal," they told me. Comparatively, this position did require the least amount of exertion, but as a team member I was still required to lap the entire football field four times before practice, as a warm up. Did I mention I hated it?

After that forgettable soccer season in middle school, the last time I remember "running," if it could even be called that, was in high school gym class. Every year we were corralled and forced outside onto the school track to complete the running portion of the Presidential Fitness Assessment. Even then, my only motivation was the potential humiliation of failing gym class. Running was not my gift. Running was not my jam. I hated it. Despite all of the hard evidence of my actual life experiences related to running, when my friend invited me to join her in that race, all I could see was my imagined self, lapping the track like Eric Liddell in the film *Chariots of Fire* (cue the slow-motion video of me running to the theme song from that film). This delusional interpretation informs what happened next. Carrie called a few months into our training to ask me if I'd be willing to run the ten-mile stretch rather than the six-miles we'd originally agreed on. I hesitated only a moment before agreeing to it.

I mean, if I could run six miles, what's four more?

Run for Your Life

The comparison of the Christian faith with running a race is no new analogy. In Hebrews, Paul used race imagery to encourage Christians who were suffering under the oppressive boot of the Roman empire. At the time of Paul's message, Christ had been crucified. In the aftermath of the resurrection, His followers endured unimaginable torture, imprisonment, and martyrdom. Paul rallies with "Let us run with endurance the race that is set before us" (Hebrews 12:1). I can almost imagine him speaking with a fist raised in the air and a fire in his eyes. He continues,

Let us also lay aside every weight, and sin which clings so closely, and let us run with endurance the race that is set before us, looking to Jesus, the founder and perfecter of our faith, who for the joy that was set before him endured the cross, despising the shame, and is seated at the right hand of the throne of God.

Hebrews 12:2-3

Paul's words here are more than a motivational speech. He is talking about life and death. Not physical life, not the life of the body, but the life of the spirit. Paul, a life-long sufferer of his own mysterious "thorn in the flesh," knew that our mortal flesh is a temporary vehicle by which we are called to live out the life of the spirit. In our physical bodies we practice obedience and good works for the sake of spreading the gospel. He wasn't encouraging the faithful at that time to run from their commitment to Christ, but rather to run forward in the life of faith, with all of the risk and cost that came with it. To push on, headlong into the face of certain death, because that is what Christ did for them. Because it is what He did for us.

Paul knew their struggle intimately. He propagated it himself, describing his pre-conversion life as a former blasphemer, persecutor, and insolent opponent (1 Timothy 1:13). Before his own conversion, Paul was party to the oppressive practices of the Roman empire.

For you have heard of my former life in Judaism, how I persecuted the church of God violently and tried to destroy it.

Galatians 1:13

He knew exactly what he was encouraging those early Christians to face. He knew how this kind of obedience would end. The "finish line" for these believers didn't include an olive leaf crown and a trophy, but a cross. Paul's image of encouragement for enduring the long-suffering of their faith is that of the surrender of Christ.

Consider him who endured from sinners such hostility against himself, so that you may not grow weary or fainthearted.

Hebrews 12:3

To say that these believers needed encouragement is a woeful understatement. How impossible it must have seemed in those days to embrace Christ, knowing that to profess your faith was to sign your own death warrant? Most of us in the West aren't facing the risk of this kind of persecution. We live with abundant freedom to practice our faith in nearly whatever way we feel inclined. This is both a gift and an obstacle to our surrender. Our freedom is our excuse. We use it to rationalize away the need to endure, to persevere, to do hard things. When pressure mounts, we are free to walk away. No one is going to drag us back to the stocks.

The no-pressure stakes of our culture weakens our endurance muscles. When the going gets tough, we become despondent and wander away. I've always been really good at starting things. But finishing them? That's a different matter. Starting is easy. There's an energy that comes in the beginning of a project that helps propel us into the work at hand. But the deeper into the work we go, the harder it is to maintain that initial energy boost. The initial "high" of accomplishment dissipates. The only way to keep going is to endure. To persevere. This is true in virtually every area of our lives that requires something of us. From parenting, to our careers, to running—endurance is the necessary ingredient if we want to finish well. Or even just finish.

"What people don't realize is how much religion costs. They think faith is a big electric blanket, when of course it is the cross. "[1]

Highs and Lows

The distance between six and ten miles is more than four. I know that sounds like bad math, but that four-mile difference changed everything. At the beginning of my training, making it six miles had seemed challenging, but not impossible. Ten miles, however, might as well have been a full marathon. Every time I stepped on the treadmill to train, I came face to face with my weakness. Though I had good form, I developed plantar fasciitis, a painful inflammation of tissue on the bottom of the feet. My knees ached, my shoulders hurt, my lungs burned and occasionally, I'd get one of those horrendous side cramps that felt like someone was stabbing me between my lower two ribs. The side cramps only happened when I didn't breathe right. Before I started running, I didn't think about how I breathed; I didn't imagine it mattered. But when you're running, all of the sudden the way you breathe becomes important. There's a rhythm to it that's unique to each runner. When you find your rhythm, when you train your lungs, you can avoid the dreaded side stitch. The more I learned about running, the more applicable Paul's metaphor became.

The only way to effectively train for a race is to build up your endurance a little at a time. The method I chose for training involved a combination of walking and running. Every couple of days, the ratio of walking to running would shorten. In addition to that, the distance would lengthen as well, until you were walking only for a warm up, and then running the remainder of the time. This is the most effective way to become a runner. The slow ramp-up helps condition your body for the long haul. I was improving. I was becoming a runner. But no matter how much I trained, the nagging reality of my weakness was ever before me. Every time I tied my shoes and stepped out of my door for a run, I felt the full weight of my inadequacy. With every footfall on the pavement, I never knew for sure if I would finish that day's required run. As dramatic as this sounds, every run became an altar I would crawl up on. Here I am, Lord. Help me, be my strength. I offer myself in all my weakness to you.

A few weeks into training, I knew that if at the end of that eight months, I did in fact make it to the finish line of that ten-mile race, it would be because I had died a hundred small deaths to get there.

If you've been around people who make a habit of running, you've probably heard them talk about the elusive and mysterious "runner's high." This strange and unexpected sensation happens when prolonged aerobic exercise results in experiencing a feeling of euphoria, coupled with a reduction in pain. I'd heard about it before, but I figured it was a bunch of bogus, runner-enthusiast voodoo talk intended to help recruit other people into the cult of running. I never believed any kind of euphoric feeling could occur while running.

But on the last long run of my training, just a couple of days before the race, I experienced it—runner's high—for myself. I was eight miles in with a mile to go, when I distinctly remember this strange warmth that coursed through my body. It was different than the warmth you feel from exertion. I was buzzing. Every molecule in my body felt electric and invincible. I felt outside of myself. I literally felt as if I could run forever, and never tire out. Having never experienced this before, I was so distracted by what I was feeling, that I took a wrong turn and got lost in my own neighborhood. I had to run an extra half-mile to course correct. When I stepped back onto my driveway, I had run a full nine-and-a-half miles.

While there's a scientific explanation for the runners high, that day, the high was an answer to prayer. Because for me, running is both boring and hard, I had used my run times as prayer times. I'd wanted to do this, but I'd also needed to. Every step for me was grueling, and prayer was both a salve and a distraction from the misery of the work my body was doing.

Prayer during my runs kept my mind focused on Mani, and the whole reason I'd said yes to this race in the first place. Training for this ten-mile race felt harder than childbirth. I'd had four babies by then, and this running thing was by far the greater challenge. While the act of running conditions the body, the mind and the heart are another matter.

While training, I discovered that running is more than a mechanical repetition of bodily motion. The mind and heart get involved, and for me, in that season, running this race was a full-body war. My post-pregnancy body was admittedly out of condition. But so, too, were my head and my heart. Every time I stepped onto the treadmill, my insecurities and fears rose up like a cobra, bearing fangs, hissing and lunging at my soul. Every single time I laced up my shoes, the war would wage:

Negative self-talk: "You're too overweight to run this race. You'll be the last across the finish line."

Excuses about why I couldn't do it (some legit, and others, pure lies): "You have too much to do today to get your run in."

Phantom pains: "Your knees are breaking with every foot-fall."

Distraction: "You're almost to Walmart—maybe you should stop in and buy some milk."

Discouragement: "Running is hard. You hate running. This is stupid. None of this will make any difference."

There were a hundred mostly legitimate reasons why I should have quit this nonsense and gotten back to my regularly scheduled life. But whenever I tried to seriously entertain thoughts about quitting, I remembered that the race wasn't about me, it was for Mani. It was for each one of those faces I'd seen on the Compassion table at our church during ministry spotlight week.

For all those months, I spent mile after mile convincing myself that I was not going to die, and that I could, in fact, keep going. The one-time runner's high just a few days before the race was a gift, because I'd wanted to quit nearly every day of the eight months of training. That final long run was critical to being able to complete the entire ten miles that loomed just days later. Only two things kept me going: the commitment I made to my friend, and the commitment I'd made to Compassion International—to our sponsored child, Mani.

I drew constant comparisons between his life in Rwanda, and my abundant life in middle America. Here I lived with an overabundance of freedom—I could run outside in the relative safety of my neighborhood, or inside, if it was too hot. I could pound down all of the post-run carbs I wanted to without worry that I'd be eating through the next week's food budget in a single meal. I could take a warm shower in clean water when I was finished with my training. I had running shoes and custom-made inserts that I purchased in a store that I'd driven to in my air-conditioned car. Every time I thought about quitting, I'd see Mani's face in my mind. It was a privilege to race for him, not a guilt trip.

Afraid To Say Yes

What so many of us fear when we think about surrender is the possibility of being asked to do hard things. If we say we are all in to God, what might He ask of us? It's an honest question. Our fears and hesitations are not without warrant. We've seen God usher willing people into difficult circumstances. We've watched people move to remote places of the globe to serve impoverished communities. We've watched people forced to retire early from a job they loved to care for aging family members. We've mumbled prayers in church for families suffering in their own small surrenders. We've read the stories about the persecuted Christians of Paul's day, and in our own time. We're not sure we have what it takes to give our whole selves over to God like that. In his book, *Finish*, Jon Acuff writes, "You've got some secret rules that make it really difficult for you to finish."[2] I think the same is true about our willingness to surrender. We've got some secret things that we're afraid to turn over, that make it really difficult for us to say "yes" to God.

The reality is that surrender does have a cost. Saying "yes" to God's plans and purposes over our own is a risky thing. We will be changed by this kind of obedience. We will likely be uncomfortable, and we will make others uncomfortable. Recovering people-pleasers like myself weigh this cost with fear and a bit of sadness. Saying "yes" to God might lead to being misunderstood and even rejected by those in our communities. What then? How will we manage? Saying "yes" to God opens up a lot of questions that have difficult answers—or no answers at all.

But the answer to these questions is a matter of perspective. If we believe God is who His Word says that He is, then the only answer must be "yes." Our willingness to surrender always comes back to what we believe about the nature of God. It's always a matter of love and trust. Do we love God? Do we trust Him?

Because we are human, and incapable of perfection, the answer to these two questions can change throughout the day, minute by minute, depending on whatever trial of obstacle we are facing right then. Our surrender can be a weeping, fearful, anxious yes. I don't think that God is honored by a false enthusiasm for what is more than likely going to be a difficult road. I don't think our surrender has to be some happy-clappy triumphant march into the unknown. Jesus' own walk to the cross was not this way. He was obedient unto death, but He wasn't giddy about it.

God does not ask us to give the perfect surrender in our strength, or by the power of our will. Our strength and ability bear no weight when it comes to surrender; "God is willing to work it in you."[3] This is the gift—we cannot do it in our own strength. We are neither expected nor required to. The very nature of surrender is the confession and admission that without Christ's help we can do nothing. *No thing.* In this state of admission, God receives our weakness and strengthens us for the task by the indwelling of His Holy Spirit, our tireless Helper. Every time we say "yes" to God, our resistance is weakened. Every small act of obedience in this way deepens our unity with God. This is what it means to be in Christ.

The morning of the race I logged into the fundraising website we'd built to see that we'd raised close to $500 for Compassion International. We hadn't quite hit our goal but now it was time to run. My personal goal apart from raising funds to support the ministry was that I would not finish last. It was a small, but achievable goal—at least that's what I hoped.

This particular race course was a there-and-back, meaning you run half the distance of the total race, and then turn around and run back to the start line. Carrie and I had decided early in the race that we'd run at our own pace, so as not to hold the other person back. I'd run the bulk of the race completely alone, only passing another runner occasionally. I hit the 5-mile marker and turned around to see no one on the course. My heart sagged. I was sure I'd be last across the finish line. Discouraged by my assumptions, I turned my attention towards praying for Mani. It helped to distract myself from the throbbing in my knees by thinking about someone else's hardships.

As I rounded the bend of the last mile, I passed a man and a couple of women lagging behind him. I waved at them, cheering them on. I wouldn't be last across the finish line. But more than that, was the fact that I would cross the finish line at all. In the last mile of the race all of the hours of my training passed before my eyes like a montage. Tears slipped down my sweaty cheeks as I thought about all of the times I'd come so close to quitting. Running had been so much harder than I imagined, and ten miles was so much farther than six. This time, surrender didn't look like being still, or resting in God's presence. This time, surrender had been a hard-scrabble push to do something that was beyond my own strength. In this, God taught me that sometimes, surrender looks more like pressing into what feels impossible, and learning to trust that God is both able and willing to carry us when we step out into hard places of obedience. Here, I discovered that the more we surrender, the more we develop a new posture. The more willing we are to say *yes* to God, the more it becomes a reflex, rather than a decision.

God, endurance is a hard discipline to develop. We are frail, fragile people. And sometimes, no matter how much we think we can, we can't, and still, You love us fully. Help us remember that surrender isn't always about standing still. Help us to know when it's time to rest in obedience, and when it's time to work. Make us people willing to do hard things for others. God be the strength in us, that this life requires. Fix our eyes on You as we run, walk and hobble through our race. Remind us that it doesn't matter when we finish, only that we keep pace with You. You'll get us across the finish line, and our place will be with You. As we remember that everything is Yours, teach us to delight in the effort, to find joy in the practice of surrender. Loosen our knees so that we bend willingly, God. In Jesus' name, amen.

7

You're Not The Only One

Our transformation is never for our sake alone. It is always for the sake of others.

Ruth Haley Barton

It's February in middle Ohio, and I am bone-crushingly tired. This whole experience is new, and even though I try not to have expectations, they creep in. Repeatedly, I remind myself that this is an act of obedience. I repeat this process in prayer, like a mantra. It's yours God, do whatever you want to do with it. I mean it, but I am also reminding myself to let it go, to trust God with it.

I'd just released my first book.

Book releases are roller-coaster rides of emotion. Thrilling, terrifying exciting, joyful, hopeful, disappointing—you have all of the feelings. You practice holding on and letting go, all at once. This is true for any project or art we make that shifts from being our private work to a public commodity. After working alone for months, you suddenly birth all of that work out into the world for the critical review and consumption of the public. You have no control over how your work will be received. It is a perfect exercise in learning to surrender. In the weeks after sending my book out into the world, I'd received multiple inquiries asking if I was hosting a retreat centered around my book. I wasn't. I would have ignored this idea except that I received multiple inquiries from unrelated people—and all of them strangers to me. While considering a retreat, a long-held dream of mine resurfaced. For years I'd wanted to go on a silent retreat, a weekend (or longer!) where participants are encouraged not to speak, and where they are minimally spoken to.

With my dream renewed by the suggestive powers of a handful of messages from strangers, I began researching monasteries. Within minutes, I found the perfect location for my personal getaway. In the middle of nowhere Arkansas, hours from the nearest airport and inconvenient to any possible distraction. *Yes, please. And it's shockingly affordable, much less than the cost of a single night in a hotel. And meals are included—I could take my hushed meals at the table with the resident monks.* It felt as if my dream might just come true. And then a stray thought interrupted my planning.

You're not the only one who wants a retreat.

I recognized the voice immediately. God's. My shoulders sagged under the weight of this thought. *But I want to go alone!* I said out loud to the walls of my bedroom. But even as I said it, I knew it was a waste of breath. I'd just walked through a season of intimate hand-holding with God in the process of writing my book. Even as I tried to resist, I knew that I wasn't going to say no to God.

"We might argue with God a bit. We might put forth every excuse that comes to mind. But God always wins this argument, because every time we go deep inside to listen, we know that what God is calling us to do is ours to do and that the path before us is ours to walk...We say yes to God."[1]

I suddenly realized that the messages I'd received inquiring about a retreat had not been as odd or random as I originally believed. With God's breath still hanging in the air, I felt more was going on than I knew.

"I believe that people laugh at coincidence as a way of relegating it to the realm of the absurd and therefore not having to take seriously the possibility that there is a lot more going on in our lives than we either know or care to know. Who can say what it is that's going on? But I suspect that part of it, anyway, is that every once and so often we hear a whisper from the wings that goes something like this: 'You've turned up in the right place at the right time.'"[2]

Those messages were "whispers from the wings." The messages had been a holy invitation. I remained still a while longer, quiet. The monks of my earlier daydream disappeared, and what emerged instead was a picture of a small gathering of women like myself—moms, sisters, friends—tired, hungry women who longed for uninterrupted time for prayer and reflection. Women just like me. I sensed in that instant what the retreat would be called— *Refine*—a nod to the unending work of the Holy Spirit in my own life, and certainly in the lives of all of my fellow pilgrims limping through their faith journey.

Whataboutery

When God asks us to do something that feels foreign, or hard, or risky, our objections fall into a few common categories. Usually, we react with a, *yeah, but whatabout...* and then fill in the blanks with our *objection du jour:*

Whatabout the fact that nobody even knows who I am? (Concern about our identity)

Whatbout people who won't like me if I do this, or whatabout if I fail? (Fear of rejection or failure)

Whatabout the fact that I don't know anything about doing this? (Lack of qualifications, skills, know-how, etc.)

Whatabout the fact that I am broke and don't have time to learn a new skill right now? (Lack of resources, financial, education, materials)

We think we're so original. We're not. That stuff's as old as Moses. When God calls to Moses from the burning bush and asks him to deliver the Israelites out of the oppressive hand of Pharaoh, Moses is overcome with self-doubt.

> But Moses said to God, "Whatabout the fact that I'm a murderer on the lam? I'm not the one to confront Pharaoh" (paraphrased, Exodus 3:11).

Moses considered himself, a murderer (Exodus 2:11-12), and estranged son to Pharaoh, and doubted that anyone would listen to him, least of all Pharaoh. Moses' objection did not dissuade God to change His mind. God's response?

> "But I will be with you"
>
> Exodus 3:12

My conversation with God sounded similar — Whatabout the fact that I've never planned more than a backyard birthday party or a family Christmas dinner? Whatabout the fact that I have zero experience planning, much less marketing an event? On paper, I lacked nearly all of the necessary qualifications for planning a retreat. I had no experience planning or selling an event. I did not know the first thing about planning something where real money would have to be exchanged, contracts signed, and hard deadlines met. I made a mental list of all of the reasons I had no business planning an event, not the least of which was that I didn't want to do it.

Our resistance to surrender is always rooted in some truth about who we are. Even those of us who usually tend towards feelings of invincibility bump up against our legitimate limitations. God calls, and we stipulate our obedience according to our intellectual and physical skills set. We refer to our Strengths Finder™ results, our

Enneagram numbers and our Meyers Briggs panel, to determine whether or not we are a good fit for whatever God is asking of us. As if He didn't create us as an ENFP, INTJ, (or whatever other letter combination we ascribe to ourselves). As if He didn't weave into the very fibers of our being, the strengths of *input, individualization,* and my personal favorite Strengths Finder™ result—*woo.*

We've always been this way. A people full of excuses. All of us—since the beginning of life outside of the Garden. Think again about when God called Moses to lead the Israelites out of slavery in Egypt. After offering up his first excuses, Moses tells God he can't do it because he is "slow of speech and tongue" (Exodus 4:10). Whether Moses had a physical speech impediment, or it was his heart that impeded his ability to say "yes" to God's ask, the point is that he resisted, more than once. Moses looked sideways at God's enormous call and told God straight up that He'd made a mistake. *I'm not your man, pick someone else.*

I don't know about you but when I sit with that for a minute, Moses' excuse-making drops like a heavy thud at my feet. I can't help but see my own b-roll of the countless times I've dared to tell God that He's chosen the wrong lady to do the thing. The times I've stood toe-to-toe with God and told Him square, You've made a mistake. Just who exactly do I think I am? Who exactly do I think God is? No one knows the intimate details secretly woven into our DNA like the Very God, who with His own hands, knit our cells together in the hidden place of our mother's womb.

For you formed my inward parts; you knitted me together in my mother's womb.

Psalm 139:13

No one is more intimately acquainted with our skills and our shortcomings, than our Father, who has witnessed our every failure and success. He has been present in every line of our story—and even before, when we were nothing more than a dream He held of us. He is well-versed in our private indulgences and the pet lies we embrace. He knows all of our usual hiding places.

Here's what we know, but don't believe: God is infinitely able to do all things. If God knows that we have no real job experience for the task He's inviting us to perform, why do we feel the need to remind Him obsessively, that we're not qualified? Why do we get on our high horse about how unskilled we are, and how hard it will be to do something we don't know how to do? God knows it's going to be difficult for us.

What we assume when God says do this or that seemingly-impossible thing is that He is asking us to do it by ourselves. In our own strength. When we start picturing the work, we see ourselves trying to figure it all out, alone. How silly we are. When God asked Moses to confront Pharaoh about his heinous treatment of the Israelites, God was saying, *come with Me. You and I are going to free My people once and for all.* Moses assumed that he was somehow supposed to do all the heavy lifting. But that was the vision of a man only capable of dreaming within the realm of the limitations of the human imagination. That wasn't God's vision for the Exodus. God's imagination is infinite. God wasn't looking for a superhero to do His bidding with Pharaoh, He was inviting Moses, an imperfect man, into an intimate relationship with Himself. Every invitation to surrender, is at the very core, this same thing—an invitation to deeper intimacy with God, where we discover what true freedom looks like.

God's invitations are always multi-layered. Our surrender—this kind of obedience (answering when we're called) —is never just for our own sake. Not exclusively. Whether we are conscious of it or not, our lives are linked to far more than our personal blood lines and immediate family units. Because "no man is an island," our actions, choices, obedience, behavior, words, decisions, spending habits, disobedience (you get the picture), will impact another person's life at some point. Even if we are unaware (as we most often are) of how that might happen, or what that might look like.

Moses didn't see himself as the man for the job because he was looking solely at himself. He based his objections on what he knew about his own abilities, in his own strength That self-centered perspective eclipsed the plight of a people who were suffering under the weight of decades of oppression. This is what happens when we fail to imagine that our personal surrender has invisible arms that stretch beyond our limited scope of perceived impact. While we're obsessively, and often cruelly, disqualifying ourselves for the invitations of God, our refusal to surrender has a reach we can't begin to fathom.

If you've read Moses' story, you know that though he *"dost protesteth much"*, he eventually accepted the mantle God invited him to carry, and led an often-contemptuous people through the wilderness. It's a difficult, sometimes comical, and often heartbreaking story. The Exodus of God's people out of Egypt reads a bit like an ancient soap opera and a Greek tragedy tangled up together. It is a story of imperfect surrender. No one makes it through unscathed—even Moses himself, who in a fit of pride and faithlessness, lost the privilege of ever setting foot in the Promised Land (Numbers 20). And yet, Moses' imperfect surrendered obedience changed the course of history forever. He is counted amongst God's faithful, and remembered as a man of God (Hebrews 3:5, Hebrews 11).

Fleece and Seeds

We didn't know what was happening, but as my little self-published book took flight into the world, it was clear that God was carrying it, as all kinds of unsolicited doors opened to opportunities to share the message. Within weeks of its release, three churches, including one internationally, wrote asking permission to use my book as their church-wide Lenten study. Other writers whom I did not know messaged me asking if I'd write a guest posts for their websites, or do an interview. Clearly whatever was happening was beyond me.

I never intended that book to be anything other than a free offering to my blog readers. Then a friend suggested that I also sell it, in the name of being a good steward of my time, money, and the effort that it took to produce the book. I considered her suggestion, and decided somewhat hesitantly that I would. Guess what? People bought the book. They could still get it for free, but people were buying it. Several thousand copies were downloaded from my website, and I watched, stunned, as sales came in and the book climbed the Amazon charts, finding its way into the top 3, then settling into the top 10 books in its category during the season of Lent. Within weeks a small, but not insignificant, nest-egg had landed in my bank account from the sales of the book. I knew without hesitation that it wasn't "mad-money" to be spent frivolously. Every dollar felt ear-marked for something. They were seeds.

In the book of Judges, Gideon twice tests God, looking for confirmation that he has indeed been called to lead the Israelite army against the Midianites. Two times, Gideon throws out a sheep's fleece, once asking God to cause the fleece to become wet overnight with dew, while the ground remains dry, and another time asking for the ground to be wet, but for the fleece to remain dry (Judges 6, 7).

Both times, God answers in the affirmative. Much to his chagrin, Gideon had heard correctly.

In an effort to see if God really meant what I'd heard Him whisper, I decided to take the fleece route. The first fleece I threw down was whether or not my husband would be receptive to this retreat idea. My husband is practical and methodical. He is not prone to fits of impulsive, reactionary behavior. He does not experience, a "word from the Lord" in the same ways that I do. In the name of matrimonial harmony, I have regularly told God that if He wants me to do something, He needs to somehow, communicate this same plan to my husband. God is the God of unity, and because I believe God loves my marriage even more than I do, I believe that if God indeed is extending an invitation to one of us, He extends it to both of us. What I mean by this is simply that if God is asking one of us to enter into something that will affect us both and our family, He unites our hearts and minds in it—or we don't move forward. Telling my husband about this wild idea, and seeing if he would bless or reject it, served as my first fleece.

To my surprise and perhaps dismay, Kurt was on board.

Hosting an event is not a free exercise. It costs real money. This was the next of my objections I presented to God. This falls under the "lack of resources" category. I began researching possible retreat locations, partly out of curiosity, and also, so I could present the ridiculousness of God's idea back to Him. I knew there was nothing affordable, and after several internet searches, I would prove it. I found a beautiful retreat facility just an hour and change from my home, but it was fully booked for the time frame I'd settled on. Second-best seemed to be a local state park that boasted a large lodge featuring not only hotel style accommodations, but conference rooms and catering. It seemed to be a near-perfect fit for the vision that was unfolding, still, I knew when I called them, it would be unaffordable. When I inquired about the cost, I learned that a substantial deposit would need to be made to reserve the site. This was the evidence I needed to tell God that His retreat idea was not going to work. The only problem was, when I looked at my bank balance from the book sales, I had enough money. In fact, I had the exact amount.

Seeds indeed.

Even with my husband on board, and an affordable facility nearby, I remained hesitant to embrace this retreat idea. I reached for another fleece. Her name is Christa. A couple of years before all of this, I'd been introduced to Christa's music at a conference. She didn't know me, but I knew her through her songs, and she was the only person who came to mind when I thought about who might lead worship at this retreat. I sent her a message pitching her this crazy idea, fully certain that one of two things would happen:

She wouldn't respond at all.
She would say "no."

I left no room for any other answer. Within hours of sending her my rambling message about this ridiculous idea for a retreat, she responded "Yes."

Nothing was happening according to my plan. Every possible door I assumed would be barred and bolted shut seemed to open wide. I knew less than nothing about planning an event like this, selling tickets, or building a program for this kind of a weekend (what were we supposed to do there anyway?), and yet everything I needed continued to find me. It was as if God Himself was hand-delivering the retreat, piece by piece. Clearly God had a purpose in mind that I knew nothing about. My only role was to keep listening and keep following.

My sheep hear my voice, and I know them, and they follow me.

John 10:27

And I know them. Don't miss that middle part of this verse. None of our objections to surrender are new to God. He knows us more intimately than we know ourselves. Before we have formulated our arguments against His cause, He has already seen the entire conversation from beginning to end. There is no objection or hesitation we can raise that God has not already accounted for. This is good news. This means that we can rest in His fore-knowledge, and simply follow where He leads. The pressure's off. We don't have to "run the show." We don't have to know the outcome.

That April, twenty-four women joined me at a state park lodge in Ohio for a weekend retreat called *Refine {the retreat}*. It altered all of our lives. After our 72 hours together, none of us were quite able to articulate what we had experienced, except to say that God had been palpably present with us. Through our worship, through art, through intentional fellowship, God brought healing, freedom and vision to the women who came. Our only role that weekend had been to show up—to say yes to God, and then let the Holy Spirit work in us.

Five years after that initial retreat, God's vision for *Refine* continues to unfold. What began as a tiny seed of an idea, is now an annual pilgrimage. Each March I take between 40-45 women on retreat with me, and every time, God does a new thing. Every year I have hosted the event, it has sold out.

In the weeks and months after the women return from *Refine*, I receive letters and messages about their experience on retreat. These letters are sacred to me. They are stones of remembrance—a generous testimony of God's kindness and faithfulness. I save each one, because even though I have hosted this event nearly five times, I'm still tempted to forget how much God can do with a willing heart. When I doubt God's provision, I have a treasure box of encouragement sent to me by women deeply impacted by what God chooses to do in and through us, when we say *yes,* when we come open and willing for whatever He has for us. Learning to listen for God's voice is about more than just hearing.

Look at that last part of John 10:27; My sheep hear my voice, and I know them, and they follow me. A surrendered heart follows the good Shepherd. When we are following in faith, the outcome doesn't even matter, God is leading.

God, interrupt our ideas and give us hearts that dream Your dreams. Everything is Yours. Teach us what it means to say "yes" to Your purposes and plans always—most especially when we think we have a better idea in mind. Help us to take leaps of faith that surrender and obedience require of us, trusting that You're right there with us, every frightening step of the way. Turn our "what if" moments into "watch this" moments—open our eyes to see You at work. God You are so good to transform our tiny dreams into something beyond our wildest imaginations. You're always doing a new thing, and how often do we not perceive it. Jesus, lead us. Help us to see that our surrender reaches beyond ourselves to serve a purpose greater than we have envisioned. You're building your Kingdom through our tiny acts of obedience—what grace it is that You'd let us participate! Help us to want to work alongside You, in your strength and for Your glory.
In Jesus' name, amen.

8

You Can't Always Get What You Want

The reason why many are still troubled, still seeking, still making little forward progress is because they haven't yet come to the end of themselves. We're still trying to give orders, and interfering with God's work within us.

A.W. Tozer

I was raised to respect God, to honor Him in speech and prayer. I was also raised to fear God. But in that raising, somehow, I missed the distinction between being afraid and being awed. Somewhere in my young mind, this came to mean that I couldn't dare be gut-level honest with God. To bare myself in that way would be disrespectful. It might even be sinful. And so, for most of my life, I prayed the refrained prayers of one who fears a God too scary to be honestly spoken to, a God too far from His Creation to hold the intimate heft of human grief. I guess you could say that what I'm saying is I prayed safe prayers. I made genuine, but tepid requests, while keeping an eye peeled for lightning strikes. I have legitimately grieved over this realization, that for most of my Christian life I didn't even know who God actually is. At least I didn't know until I knew, until the face-in-the-carpet incident in my closet. That was the day everything changed. And I mean everything.

My face-first-in-the-carpet moment? Sure, let me explain. It had been a long season of grieving and wrestling with God. I was also seeing a professional counselor for the first time in my life. I did not come to counseling easily. I resisted the thought of a total stranger sifting through my private rubble, even as I knew I needed it. At the same time, for several months I'd been working hard on a long writing project that had come about serendipitously. Through a series of events, none initiated by me, the doors to a publishing opportunity opened, as if being held for me by an invisible hand. I practically tripped over special invitations and opportunities that were literally the answers to a handful of my private prayers. It felt as if God was rolling out an invisible red carpet for me. I couldn't believe His generosity.

I didn't see it then, but the circumstances that led to this opportunity had caused me to adopt an unspoken series of expectations. I expected the doors that God had opened leading up to this opportunity would remain wide open. I expected that while I'd have to work hard, I would eventually make it to the finish line, which in this case meant that my dream of writing a book would come true. I mean, that sounds only fair, doesn't it?

God In My Closet

I submitted my proposal to the editor, only to receive an automatic reply letting me know she'd be out of the office for a couple of weeks. *Lord give me patience,* I prayed. I'd heard that proposal review process could be slow, but after six weeks of silence, this seemed excessive. I did not wait well. Those six weeks became a spiritual battlefield as I wrestled doubts, insecurities, and fears about what feedback I might receive. As my anxiety grew, what had been a sense of awe at what God seemed to be doing turned dark, into something uglier—a sense of entitlement. The tone of my prayers shifted from hopeful expectancy to whining and desperate. Instead of giving thanks to have even had the opportunity at all, I became resentful about the seeming-slowness of God. Why did He let this happen? Why does it have to take so long? Why would He get my hopes up then leave me here with no response? Why? Why? Why?

Dear God,

I don't like You.

Love, Kris

I know how this sounds. I'm embarrassed. It sounds so shallow. Thankfully, even our shallowest, dry seasons are fertile ground to the Lord. In learning to surrender, we also discover that no matter how far we've wandered, we are never out of God's reach. God has the mystifying ability to work within our hearts, no matter how cracked or ugly they may appear. As Leonard Cohen famously sang, "There's a crack in everything. That's how the Light gets in."[1] And it's not just the Light that slips into these cracks. The cracks are also the places where God's "refining fires" are kindled. It's as if God presses His lips against our mottled hearts, blowing His Holy breath into the cracks. He ignites a spark and the same breath that filled Adam's lungs *in the beginning*, fans the flames.

The morning of the beginning of the seventh week of waiting, I stood in the entrance of my closet. I wasn't trying to decide on what to wear. I wasn't looking for a lost shoe. I was raging—quietly, but still raging. Something was wrong with me. I'd lost all hope of receiving a positive response about my project. I knew the answer from the editor—whenever it finally arrived—would be "no." This thought settled so solid in my gut that it knocked the wind out of me. This was not self-doubt speaking. This was not coming from myself at all.

"Get on your face."

I heard the words as clear as if they were spoken directly into my ear. My knees stiffened. I will not. But then, as if directed by an invisible force, even as my spirit resisted, my physical body folded over onto itself. With my face buried in the dust of the carpet, my knees scrunched beneath me, I knew: "Surely the presence of the Lord was in this place."[2] Against my own stubbornness, tears spilled out of my eyes. I growled angry, rebuking words at God. *Why are you crushing the dreams you awakened in me? What kind of a God are you? I'm so angry at you!* As a deep grief worked its way up from my toes, my growling turned to heaving sobs. This was the ugliest of ugly cries. And then, in the middle of my breakdown, a breakthrough. An inexplicable sensation flooded my heart. Mingled with my grief and disappointment, a gentle warmth flooded my veins. Even as I pummeled God with my bitter prayers, in what was surely one of my ugliest, most unlovely moments, I felt overwhelmingly loved.

Imagine being held by the person you love most in the world. That sweetness, that security you feel with their arms wrapped around you—that's what I felt as I shook and spit my hurt at God. It made no sense, but it was as real a moment as this one now, writing these words here.

In my spirit, it was as if I heard God encouraging me to say more. It seemed like He was saying, *"C'mon, Kris. Is that all you've got?"* The more fire I breathed His direction, the more that feeling of being held intensified. When I'd exhausted myself, I lay still on my face. As my tears slowed a thought came to mind. None of the venom I spewed at God caught Him by surprise. When I said earlier that after that face-first-in-the-closet moment everything changed? What I meant was I changed.

I'm an open book to you; even from a distance, you know what I'm thinking. You know when I leave and when I get back; I'm never out of your sight. You know everything I'm going to say before I start the first sentence.

Psalm 139: 2-4, Msg

Later that week, after I'd wrestled with God in the privacy of my closet, the email I'd been waiting for from the editor arrived in my inbox. Indeed, it was a hard "no"—just as I'd heard it would be that day in my bedroom. After months of work and waiting, the doors to that dream slammed shut. Poof. Just like that. *You shall not pass.*[3]

Maybe you have had hard seasons like the one I describe here. Maybe your dream wasn't a book, but a baby. Maybe your dream was a marriage that would last instead of one that ended in betrayal, or the devastation of divorce. Maybe it was a steady job rather than an unending unemployment line.

For some of us, the dream-now-crushed is for health, when instead we're sitting beneath a stack of medical bills threatening to bury us in our still-undiagnosed state. If you've ever been stunned by the ways the Lord giveth and taketh away,[4] then you know how these temporal situations can feel like an eternal hell. It isn't fair—because life isn't fair. *Fair* isn't a word in God's economy. God's not a genie, He's no fairy godfather. But He is a good Father who instead of granting wishes, loves us into new creations.

Sometimes He loves us by saying no. This is what good parents do, they sometimes say no to the demands of their children because they have the long view of the child's life in mind. The parent knows that some things, no matter how strongly desired or insisted upon, are not in the child's best interest. A hard *no* from God is a most loving response.

In the heat of God's love, the chaff of our life burns away. The dreams we've prayed or begged for are sifted like wheat. In the fire of His refining mercy, our hearts are literally transformed. When we let Him humble us, we can become what we are destined to be.

The humbling of God is the healing of God. But it doesn't always feel like it. Sifting wounds our pride. It brings out the little tyrant-toddler in our hearts that has never fully grown up. And since the root of all sin is pride, we're all carriers of the same infection, to varying degrees. During that hard-humbling season, I had become sick, and I had no idea just how sick I was. Self-righteous, prideful living is soul-rot, ruining us from the inside out. The cure, of course, is repentance.

You Get What You Need

Do you remember the story of Naaman? He didn't wrestle God in his closet, but he had a similar struggle. Though he enjoyed favor and notoriety for his brilliant command of the Syrian army, he was sick with leprosy. But God had it in mind to heal him. As it turned out, a recent raid in Israel included the capture of a girl who had become a servant to Naaman's wife. The young girl, knowing Naaman's situation, claimed that there was a man in Israel, a prophet named Elisha, who could heal him.

So Naaman came with his horses and chariots and stood at the door of Elisha's house. And Elisha sent a messenger to him, saying, "Go and wash in the Jordan seven times, and your flesh shall be restored, and you shall be clean."

2 Kings 5:9-10

This seemed like it should have been good news. Elisha had given Naaman the prescription that he desperately wanted. But Naaman wasn't having it. Rather than joyful obedience or surrender, Naaman scoffed at God's method. He got angry. "Behold, I thought that he would surely come out to me and stand and call upon the name of the Lord his God, and wave his hand over the place and cure the leper" (2 Kings 5:11).

Naaman had expectations. He wanted healing, but he wanted it a particular way. He wanted the spectacular, the fanfare of the miraculous, to call on God like one might whistle for a servant, and receive the miracle. Rather than receive word from one of Elisha's servants, He wanted to see this prophet in person, to be greeted and perhaps acknowledged in esteem. He wanted to stand there and witness the spectacle of God's mighty, healing hand wave over him. Naaman objected to both the method necessary for his healing, and the location as well. He believed the waters of Damascus, in the land he had recently pillaged, to be superior to the waters in Israel.

"Are not Abana and Pharpar, the rivers of Damascus, better than all the waters of Israel? Could I not wash in them and be clean?" So he turned and went away in a rage."

2 Kings 5:12

This story is ridiculous. Who has an opportunity to be healed from leprosy and then balks at the method? There was no other existing cure for what Naaman had and for a moment there, it appears he was willing to remain a leper rather than receive the healing God had in mind. I say it's ridiculous—except for the fact that I can relate all-too-well. In the refining season God walked me through, Naaman had nothing on me. I was the one who resisted and grit my teeth in the face of surrender. I was the one who expected God to meet my expectations and desires. And when He didn't, I raged.

Can you relate? When is the last time your expectations didn't line-up with reality? How did you react?

God could have turned in that moment of arrogance and left Naaman alone in his leprosy. He certainly didn't deserve the healing he was now resisting. So, too, could God could have left me in my angry mess, there on the floor of my closet. I behaved horribly towards Him. I did not deserve the healing and hope He gave me in the days following my closet experience. Naaman wanted healing, but he was disgusted to have had to go to the place of his enemy, and be told then to wash in the filthy waters of a place he despised in order to receive what he was after. In his pride he nearly missed the miracle. I wonder how many of God's gifts I have missed in my resistance to surrender? How many times do we forsake the Good Father's "no" because it feels like punishment?

Fortunately for Naaman, his servants, who were no doubt more accustomed to obedient living simply because of their societal positioning, couldn't understand why Naaman was nearly willing to leave and take his leprous self back to Syria. Unhealed.

> But his servants came near and said to him, "My father, it is a great word the prophet has spoken to you; will you not do it? Has he actually said to you, 'Wash, and be clean?'"

2 Kings 5:13

I can hear the shock in their voices as they recount what Elisha told Naaman. "There is a way for you to be healed! Will you actually not go through with it?" God's intention was both to heal and humble Naaman. He had set into place all of the right people at the exact right time. From the captured Israelite girl, to the servants who would be there to speak wisdom and encouragement to Naaman at a critical moment, God's loving *no* was actually a beautiful *yes*. And so it was with my own surrender moment in my closet.

If we can choose a memory of a time when we felt God calling us to bend, we will likely see other people and factors at play that served to help us to our knees. Whether or not we noticed them at the time is less relevant than the fact that God supplies what we need. Finally, Naaman relents. He surrenders himself to the presumed humiliation of washing seven times in the Jordan and "he was clean" (2 Kings 5:14).

Wash and Be Clean

After Naaman's surrender, he confesses his new faith to the one true God. Then he returned to the man of God, he and all his company, and he came and stood before him. And he said,

"Behold, I know that there is no God in all the earth but in Israel; so accept now a present from your servant."

2 Kings 5:15

It's hard to argue when you get what you need.

When I pushed back against God's humbling, rather than condemnation and rejection, God drew near to me. Rather than leave Naaman sick, God was patient with him waiting for him to go to the Jordan and dip himself the seven times required. One of the most challenging aspects of learning to surrender is that true surrender requires us to lay aside our expectations.

Surrender is only ever on God's terms.

This is true, regardless of what is being asked of us. Becoming a "living sacrifice" isn't something we can endure while pushing for our own agenda, by our own parameters. It's worship, and we can only rightly worship when we remember our position to God. Our pride most often acts as a hindrance to assuming our proper position. Humility is a foreign land that speaks a language we do not know.

Naaman needed a miracle. He went willing, but hemmed in by his own preconceived notions of what that miracle should look like. We live seasons like this–burdened with expectations, so heavy laden with dreams of our own making, that we're nearly willing to walk away from the miraculous because it comes in ways we hadn't anticipated, in ways perhaps that even disappoint us.

This is not a new story, not a new struggle. Israel wanted a savior, they wanted a king, royal and regal. What God gave the world was a baby born in dirt to a couple of no prestige. Expectations eclipsed the miracle. They failed to recognize their long-desired King, as he rode in on a donkey rather than a chariot pulled by thoroughbreds.

"Just as a servant knows that he must first obey his master in all things, so the surrender to an implicit and unquestionable obedience must become the essential characteristic of our lives."[5]

Naaman got the healing he needed. In fact, God healed him from the outside-in. Naaman left to return to his duties with a load of soil in tow, so that he could build an altar on which he would now worship God for the rest of his days (2 Kings 5:17).

That day in my closet, God healed me, too. I didn't miraculously get that book contract that I wanted. What God gave me was a gift worth so much more. I had an encounter with grace. I brought my whole, ugly heart to God and He accepted it, just as it was. Where I expected rejection, I was enveloped in mercy. Where I expected a harsh reproof, I found comfort and gentle correction.

I have this sign hanging in my guest bedroom that reads "It's Your mercy that waits for us to want You." As soon as I saw it, I knew I had to have it because it perfectly describes the kindness of God that I experienced that day with my face on the floor. God was patient with Naaman, and He was patient with me. He will be patient with you too.

Gracious God, Your mercy knows no limits. Though we may resist the heat of Your refining love, help us to believe that the purification our hearts so desperately need is worth the pain of letting You in to the deepest places of our dreams, longings, desires and our fears. Hold our hands God, as You walk us into the hard places of Your perfect love. Breathe new life into our lungs, wash us clean, that we might emerge healed and restored. Help us to remember that even when You don't give us what we want, You always give us what we need; You always give us Yourself. And above all, You are a good Father. Teach us to trust that Your "no's" are a kindness, whether we understand it or not, or even like it. In Your mercy, God, loosen our grip on the flimsy things of this world that will pass away, and bring us into deeper communion with You—that we might enjoy an everlasting intimacy in Your presence that cannot be shaken or taken away. Though our dreams and expectations may be shattered, help us to remember that everything is Yours. Become for us what we long for most. In Jesus' name, Amen.

9

Struck Down But Not Destroyed

God's love does not rescue us from life's pain. It strengthens us, like the light of day strengthens every plant along the valley floor, to endure. As we endure, we mature. Our character grows. And somewhere in the hushed cold of the twilight we blossom.

Timothy Willard

I'll never forget my 14th birthday. We mark special celebrations such as this by receiving gifts, but I remember that birthday as the time when nearly everything was taken away. Meteorologists nationwide eyeing the hurricane all had said the same thing—the devastation would be catastrophic—evacuate immediately. As my friend's parents arrived to pick them up from a sleepover I'd had for my birthday, we began packing the house and our cars for evacuation. Our frequent military moves had taught us how to settle into a place quickly, and also, how to uproot at a moment's notice. With choreographed efficiency, we went through the house, room by room, evaluating our things based on their importance to us. We'd stuffed into suitcases and duffle bags, the most precious of our belongings, cramming them into the back of our station wagon. Amongst my treasured items were my journals, my favorite outfits, my pillow, a cardboard box of photos, my beloved stuffed dog, *LeMutt.* Other favorite items, like my coveted clear plastic telephone, and irreplaceable keepsakes, like my old dance recital costumes, were left behind.

What we couldn't bring with us, but hoped to save from the impending devastation, we had wrapped in large trash bags to protect it from water damage. Grabbing the cat, the parakeet, and hamsters, we'd locked the side door to the house one final time.

Accepting our limitations, and letting go of what is important to us isn't as easy as we like to imagine.

We spent that sweltering afternoon awaiting Hurricane Andrew's arrival camped at my Grandfather's old gravel-roofed, single-story, 1950's home in south Miami. His stout, rambler had stood steady through other hurricanes and tropical storms commonly experienced in that area. Her record was trustworthy. We believed we were safe. In the hours just before the storm, we passed the time eating up my birthday cake and ice cream—always the first casualty of a power outage. We'd taken turns forecasting our expectations. We'd watched hours of news coverage, and though our faith was nominal at best, I imagine my parents prayed. Though the sun still shone outside, the hurricane shutters covering the windows had made the house a tomb. The only remaining light in the house spilled from my Grandfather's antique lamps, glowing in small pools on table tops, across the curled arm of the sofa, and on the lacquered brick floors. We'd huddled in this artificial light with our Mad-libs® and our board games, trying to play but distracted by the impending storm.

That "calm before the storm" is a real phenomenon. The usual chatter of the natural world ceased. The birds had all hushed and flown. The palm fronds hung limp from their towering heights. The air barely stirred.

Passing time before a catastrophe is a strange thing.

Sometime in the night we lost power. The temperature in the house rose, as the winds roared over our heads, like a freight train barreling straight through. The metal shutters made it impossible to see out of the bedroom windows, so we let our imaginations run wild with the soundtrack of the storm booming in our ears. By 1 a.m. we huddled in the hallway—kids, parents, hamsters, cats. We sat with our backs pressed into the walls, holding flashlights and pillows in our laps, fighting to stay awake but dozing out of exhaustion.

Surrender isn't always a choice we get to make.

In the following days, my parents made the treacherous trip across town back to our home. The downed trees, splintered telephone poles, and rubble had turned the once-familiar landscape into a foreign country. Street signs littered the roads. Any recognizable landmarks left standing stood like empty shells scattered on a beach. Every devastated scene they passed on the way to our house foreshadowed what was to come.

My parents returned to find a locked door and blown out windows in nearly every room. The sliding glass door on the back of the house stood only as a frame, wide open now in a sea of glass and debris. Some stranger's patio furniture had blown through it, creating a breezeway into what used to be our dining area. In some places, the roof had been peeled back like the lid of a can. In other rooms, it was as if some huge fist had punched through making a grab at what was inside. Items hung suspended from the ceiling, as if they'd been sucked up by some giant hoover, only to get wedged between the roof beams. The refrigerator doors hung open, our groceries spoiled and rotting in the August heat.

Nearly everything in the house had been washed in seawater. Flecks of tar, glass splinters, grass, torn roof shingles and other unidentifiable debris, coated much of what we had left behind. Everything comfortable, familiar and safe had been scattered with the winds. In a few short hours, our whole life became fragmented, chipped and broken.

It was catastrophic, just as the weathermen had predicted.

My family would return only one other time to our home to pick through the remains of our belongings before it was condemned—but not before the looters had sifted through our things and taken what they'd wanted for themselves.

You're Gonna Have Trouble

One of the most uncomfortable promises found in scripture is the promise of pain: "In this world you will have trouble" (John 16:33 NIV, *emphasis added*).

Repeatedly, God's word references the inevitable, unavoidable pain of living here on earth. Because of sin, the whole world suffers regardless of faith or creed. And it's not only our groans that echo in the wind, but the whole of creation groans with us in eager anticipation of redemption (Romans 8:19-21).

Furthermore, all who desire to live a godly life in Christ Jesus will be persecuted (2 Timothy 3:12). But for Jesus' followers, suffering is more than a by-product of sin. What the enemy of our souls has intended for destruction is the very avenue through which God enters our lives (Genesis 50:20). The suffering promised to God's people is a means of grace.

The Spirit himself bears witness with our spirit that we are children of God, and if children, then heirs—heirs of God and fellow heirs with Christ, provided we suffer with him in order that we may also be glorified with him.

Romans 8:16-17

"Do not be surprised when fiery trial comes upon you to test you, as though something strange were happening to you."

1 Peter 4:12

In other words, expect to suffer. "Suffering is universal...life is terminal."[1] The Old Testament story of Job offers us one of the most tragic stories of suffering ever recorded. Just 13 verses into the story, and Job has lost nearly everything he ever had and loved. In a scene almost absurd in its devastation, we hear of the loss of Job's livestock, his servants, all of his children and their home.

Now there was a day when his sons and daughters were eating and drinking wine in their oldest brother's house, and there came a messenger to Job and said, "The oxen were plowing and the donkeys feeding beside them, and the Sabeans fell upon them and took them and struck down the servants with the edge of the sword, and I alone have escaped to tell you." While he was yet speaking, there came another and said, "The fire of God fell from heaven and burned up the sheep and the servants and consumed them, and I alone have escaped to tell you." While he was yet speaking, there came another and said, "The Chaldeans formed three groups and made a raid on the camels and took them and struck down the servants with the edge of the sword, and I alone have escaped to tell you." While he was yet speaking, there came another and said, "Your sons and daughters were eating and drinking wine in their oldest brother's house, and behold, a great wind came across the wilderness and struck the four corners of the house, and it fell upon the young people, and they are dead, and I alone have escaped to tell you."

Job 1:13-19

You would think it couldn't get any worse. But it does. In a stunning blow, Job falls sick with an illness that leaves him covered head-to-toe in painful sores (Job 2:7). In his grief, Job collapses in a heap in the dust.

And he took a piece of broken pottery with which to scrape himself while he sat in the ashes.

Job 2:8

What a visual—sitting in the ashes, the rubble, the what's-left-of-our-lives. When tragedy blindsides us, many of us collapse, just like Job. For some of us, our reaction mimics that of a wounded animal. We lash out in anger, we become indignant when others try to offer help or encouragement. We wrap our wounds around us like a smothering blanket. Some of us armor up, steeling ourselves against the pain. Others of us shut down. We lie down in despair. We turn on God, hurling blame to heaven, while reminiscing about how good our life was before God caused us such misery. Isn't this what we saw in the story of the Israelites making their way from slavery to the Promised Land? How many times did they accuse God of leading them into the wilderness to die?

Suffering has a way of warping our perspective. None of us likes to feel cornered into surrender, but "pain insists on being attended to."[2] When affliction shakes us to our foundation, we have a choice: allow ourselves to be moved by God in our suffering, or resist His mercy in the midst. C.S. Lewis famously wrote that God "shouts in our pain: it is His megaphone to rouse a deaf world..." He adds, "No doubt pain as God's megaphone is a terrible instrument..."[3] Those of us who have been rattled to our teeth by the deafening blast of this megaphone know how terrible it truly is.

One of the reasons we find Job's story particularly troubling is the fact that Job is described as a "blameless and upright man who fears God and turns away from evil" (Job 1:8). By all appearances, Job seems to be living a life of obedience to God. More frustrating perhaps than this is the fact that by the end of the story, we still don't know why God allowed Job to suffer as He did. Often this is true in our own suffering, we aren't privy to the why of our own devastations. Entire books have been written on the subject of why God allows bad things to happen to good people. But maybe, the why is not as important as we think it is.

What if, instead of shaking our fists and demanding an explanation, we looked for what God does in our suffering? What if, rather than chasing that ever elusive "why?," we turned our energy towards learning news ways of faithfulness in difficulty?

What if we saw the trouble of our lives as an invitation to a more intentional, intimate relationship with our God? What if, in the midst of our heartbreak, we actually invited God more fully into our pain rather than rejecting Him because of it? What if, in our grief, we surrendered our baggage—all of it—all of ourselves, to Him? Isn't this what we are called to? Isn't this what it means when Paul tells us to submit ourselves as a living sacrifice (Romans 12:1)?

Suffering drags us out of our comfortable places of self-sufficiency. It lays us bare, revealing to us both our great lack and our most desperate need. Our chronic self-sufficiency causes us to forget how desperately we need God in every moment, not only the hard ones.

When Job questions God in the midst of His grief, God reminds Job of his frailty. It is God who formed the seas, commands the wind. God's treatise on His Divine power and majesty in the 38th chapter of Job reminds us in no uncertain terms that God, the Creator and Origin of all things, is over His creation. And as His created beings, our role is to surrender in entirety to Him. All that we are, all that we have, all that we imagine is ours, belongs to Him. God rouses us with pain from our places of distraction because for so many of us, we cannot hear Him otherwise.

Nothing roots out our idols or upends our false theology like being brought to our knees in anguish. "The human spirit will not even begin to try to surrender self-will as long as all seems to be well with it."[4] God answers Job's why questions with a Who.

Who has cleft a channel for the torrents of rain and a way for the thunderbolt, ... From whose womb did the ice come forth, ...Who has given birth to the frost of heaven? Who has put wisdom in the inward parts or given understanding to the mind? Who can number the clouds by wisdom? Or who can tilt the waterskins of the heavens, ... Who provides for the raven its prey, when its young ones cry to God for help, and wander about for lack of food?

Job 38

In our suffering, why is a distraction—what we are to look for is *Who*. We suffer because Christ suffered. God's word is clear—our suffering is intended to teach us utter and total reliance on the Father. Suffering well leads us to complete surrender, making us more like Christ Himself, who came not to do His own will, but the will of the Father (John 6:38). Our highest aim is to be like Christ. This transformation is impossible apart from enduring suffering.

We are afflicted in every way, but not crushed; perplexed, but not driven to despair; persecuted, but not forsaken; struck down, but not destroyed; always carrying in the body the death of Jesus, so that the life of Jesus may also be manifested in our bodies. For we who live are always being given over to death for Jesus' sake, so that the life of Jesus also may be manifested in our mortal flesh. So death is at work in us, but life in you.

2 Corinthians 4:8-12

What we come face to face with in the midst of tragedy and loss is our own insufficiency. God's response to Job highlights our own smallness in light of His majesty. We have no "get-out-of-suffering" card we can play. We cannot force the goodwill we hunger for to be ours. We cannot, contrary to feel-good-pop-psychology, make our own dreams come true. We live in a sin-stained world, at the mercy of circumstances and situations beyond our control. Accidents occur. Abuse happens. Infertility binds our bodies. Layoffs rip the security of steady income from beneath our feet. Houses burn down while we sleep or storms tear down our beautifully decorated sanctuaries. Our children are taken from us. Our loved ones battle terrible diseases, only to die ravaged by their illness. We cannot prevent these things. We're gonna have trouble.

Stewarding Our Pain

Pain is, as Lewis called it, a terrible instrument. We don't like it, we don't want it. We don't think we need it. We question God's goodness in the midst of our anguish. But that is because we cannot see all that God sees. Our human perspective limits us— we do not know what is yet to come. We cannot know the ways that God intends to redeem our hurts, but must trust in faith, that He will, because He promised to do so, through His own suffering, death and resurrection. "The core of the Christian life is to live by faith."[5]

Even as I write these words I confess my own tendency to bury my pain or seek to avoid it. I make every effort to live carefully. But Frederick Buechner writes that to bury whatever it is that the world gives you, and then live as carefully as you can, is not really living at all.[6] Instead, he says we can learn to steward our pain. Buechner knows what he's talking about. He lost his own father to suicide when Frederick was just a boy. Our painful experiences are an invitation to seek the Lord. To pursue Him where He may be found and hold out our hands to Him—an invitation to offer all that we feel is left of us, so that we can accept more of Him. "The one thing a clenched fist cannot do is accept."[7] I say this not as one who has mastered this kind of open-handed living, but I have, by God's grace, experienced the release of this kind of surrender.

Surrender is where we discover the freedom of being *in* Christ. When we decrease, He increases in us. Our broken places need not become anchors tethering us to earthly ideas about loss. Stewarding our pain simply means putting it to good use—not wasting it. To steward the hardship of this life means that we open our eyes to see beyond it, that rather than fixating on the ache, we look for redemptive purpose in it. God is *always*, at all times, making *all things* new. Resurrection is not a pipe dream, it's a promise.

Stewarding our pain requires us to learn to see it with spiritual eyes, to remember, as Paul writes, suffering is an opportunity for us to rely on God who raises the dead, rather than on ourselves (2 Corinthians 1:9).

Refined and Re-defined

Since as early as the 15th century, the Japanese have been practicing the art of repairing broken things, by using a method called Kintsugi, or Kintsukuroi. "Literally translated this means *golden joinery or golden repair.'*[8] The art of Kinstugi involves the piecing together of what is broken, traditionally, pottery or dishware, with a gold or silver epoxy. Rather than attempting to hide the cracks in the repair, they are instead, highlighted by the brilliant shine of gold or silver. The piece, once broken and seemingly lost, is now re-defined as a treasure. The breaking is put to purpose. The piece quite literally has a new life—*resurrection*.

No one looks at this once-broken bowl and asks why it broke. Rather they ask who fixed it. They want to know about the Craftsman behind the restoration.

In the aftermath of the hurricane that took our home and belongings, we were forced to relocate to a new town. We found a house in a quiet neighborhood, convenient to everything and just around the corner from a little white church that sat tucked up on a hill, surrounded by a thicket of trees. You couldn't see the church from the street, but the small white sign at the base of the entrance caught our eye one day, and on Sunday, my family filled a pew in that hidden church. Before long, my siblings and I became active in the youth group there. A while later, my parents joined the choir, and before any of us knew what was happening, we found Christ—all five of us.

The hurricane that had shattered and forever altered our material lives also upended our starving spiritual lives. Before the storm, we had been regular churchgoers, nominal Christians at best, content to check the boxes of church attendance and mealtime prayers, but without any real knowledge of the person of Christ. He had been for us a cardboard cut-out. A flat Jesus, as dull and lifeless as a drawing in a children's Bible. But in the little white church hidden on the hill, our lives were forever transformed by a living God we'd heard about all of our lives, but had never known. Out of the ashes we found freedom. We experienced resurrection. The loss of our belongings had been devastating, but how could we compare that loss to the realization that the greater loss had been our spiritual starvation? We had lived so many years in the comfortable wilderness of our self-sufficiency, surrendered to no one. We needed to lose it all to find the one thing we didn't know we lacked. The false things needed to be shattered.

"Life can only be understood looking backward. It must be lived forward."[9]

Of course, this insight is only seen in hindsight. We had to endure being broken by the storm, and learn to live on the other side of it before we would ever discover this one invitation that came through devastation. We had to come face to face with our cracks and stare down into the pit of our various holes. We had to accept the refining that comes when circumstances press us out to the edges of ourselves.

This is what resurrection looks like—God tenderly picks us up from the ashes. He lifts us from the rubble, and gently puts us back together—but not as we were. The pain that has refined us is re-defined.

Jesus, You are a man of sorrows, well acquainted with suffering and grief in ways we can only barely imagine. This is hard for us to remember when our own tragedies choke the prayers in our hearts and numb our lips with despair. And still, Your suffering for our sake, becomes the fabric of the banner of love that hangs over us. You have carried the weight of the whole world, and so we can trust that the heft of our personal heartbreak is not too much for You. Everything is Yours. Help us to let You hold our hurts, Lord. Help us to release what feels lost into Your hands. Help us to trust you with our fragile and cracked up places. In the rubble of our lives, God, rebuild us. Restore us to Yourself and to the life you have given us. Help us to trust that You're filling the cracks with Yourself, and that in the re-making, we will encounter You in new ways. Give us vision for Your purpose, that we may find new life in You.
In Jesus' name, Amen.

10

All Things New

"God can do a lot with our willingness to be willing."[1]

Carolyn Arends

A few years ago, I found myself with a coveted ticket to a small conference outside of Nashville, Tennessee. Months before, when I'd purchased my ticket, I had no way of knowing how much I'd need that weekend away. I stayed with a friend of a friend, tucked upstairs in her secluded guest bedroom. Leading up to the conference, I had deliberately told almost no one that I was going to this event, in hopes of avoiding the pressure of obligatory meet-ups that happen when you're in a town populated with friends and acquaintances. I felt like I was hiding.

Ok, I was hiding. But there was a reason.

The weekend of the conference aligned with the end of a self-imposed forty-day fast from social media. Fasting in its various forms is a critical act of surrender that teaches us again and again what it means to decrease in order to see God increase (John 3:30). Fasting is a way of opening tightly laced fingers to the movement of God. It's uncomfortable, it's vulnerable, it almost always hurts before it heals. Fasting is not easy, and sometimes seems to provoke a legitimate spiritual wrestling. I come to most of my fasts with a bit of reluctance and with my hands closed. I want to do it, but it's a lot of work. I know it's not going to be easy. Did I mention forty days is a long time?

"There is a part of you that is eager, ready for anything in God. But there's another part that's as lazy as an old dog sleeping by the fire."

Matthew 26:41, MSG

This had been a particularly difficult fast. For thirty-plus days (it felt like one hundred), God had been busy poking around in my propensity for people-pleasing, revealing ways I craved and chased the approval of my peers rather than resting in my identity as God's beloved. Once again, He was shining a spotlight on my well-disguised idols.

Grief and fasting tend to go hand-in-hand. This is as it ought to be. True repentance happens when we see how our sin separates us from God. If our hearts are tender towards redemption, we will feel the sting of our own waywardness. This is good. This is right. This is the grief that heals. Transformation is painful, there's no good reason to pretend it doesn't hurt. There will be no special crowns awarded in heaven for stoicism. Fasting is a soul check-up. When we set aside our preoccupation with other things in order to spend more focused time with our Great Healer, He is kind to diagnose us and restore us. Thankfully, it's because of our chronic sin-sickness that God invites us to meet Him in the wilderness of release.

The temptation for some of us to resist surrender can be in our inability to get it right the first time, or any time for that matter. I have sworn up and down that I don't struggle with perfectionism, but my ongoing wrestling with surrender proves otherwise. When it comes to spiritual matters, I have wanted to nail it—to do it with excellence, to do it perfectly. Isn't that what we are called to? — "You therefore must be perfect, as your heavenly Father is perfect" (Matthew 5:48).

But hold on a minute. It turns out that perfection, as in without flaw, is not what Jesus is talking about here. The word *perfect* is translated from the Greek word *telos* which means "complete." Jesus isn't asking for our perfect surrender. His command is an invitation to us to be complete people. To be whole, by becoming *wholly* His.

Our flesh may resist, but it is Christ-in-us who opens our hands. It's not as complicated as we make it out to be. Becoming whole in Christ requires us to let go of the things that separate us from Him. I'd forgotten that fasting, even when done imperfectly, leads to letting go of something. Sometimes it's not even the thing we thought we might need to lose. God honors our offering, however bruised it is. Surrender means we will die a thousand little deaths in this life for the sake of finding our truest life in Christ. Out of His great sacrificial love, Christ gave Himself up for us, a fragrant offering and sacrifice to God (Ephesians 5:2). We can release our lives to Him because in His great mercy, He has shown us how.

"To love the Lord my God with all my soul will involve a spiritual cost. I'll have to give Him my heart, and let Him love through it whom and how He wills, even if this seems at times to break my heart."[2]

Loving God with every fiber of our soul inevitably means we will grieve the things we feel like we are losing. But we do not grieve as the world grieves. Our grief is tempered by the eternal hope that we know is ours because of Christ. Peter calls our hope a "living hope," a hope that survives testing by the fire of life's trials. Our hope is "living" because it is rooted in the promise of resurrection, it is rooted in Christ, who shed the grave clothes and lives now, in us, by the indwelling of the Holy Spirit (John 14:17).

According to his great mercy, he has caused us to be born again to a living hope through the resurrection of Jesus Christ from the dead, to an inheritance that is imperishable, undefiled, and unfading, kept in heaven for you, who by God's power are being guarded through faith for a salvation ready to be revealed in the last time. In this you rejoice, though now for a little while, if necessary, you have been grieved by various trials, so that the tested genuineness of your faith—more precious than gold that perishes though it is tested by fire—may be found to result in praise and glory and honor at the revelation of Jesus Christ.

1 Peter 1:3-7

Dancing in the Streets

On day two of the conference I sat in on a session called "Good Grief." The panel of speakers reflected on the need to give room for grief and lament to run their course in our lives. It was day thirty-nine of my fast, and given my own private grief at the moment, I needed an encouraging word about how my quiet suffering could be good. One of the speakers, Carrie, talked about the often difficult to describe intermingling of grief and joy. The visual she shared for this mix was the Jazz Funeral.

As tradition goes, during a Jazz funeral, the procession to the church begins with hymns or spirituals played in low notes, an expected and appropriate soundtrack to accompany the grieving on their way to the service. This somber series of songs continues from the church to the cemetery, as guests walk slowly down the streets. But once the body has been released to the grave, something unexpected happens. The tone of the music shifts. The blues-infused dirge of that initial procession now picks up its tempo. Instead of walking with heads down, the mourners now saunter. They skip. They hop in time to the music, walk-dancing their way out of the graveyard. They clap their hands at their waists or with arms raised above their heads. They whoop and celebrate, spinning their parasols and waving their handkerchiefs in the air. Arms wide, they wave in on-lookers, inviting them to join the funeral procession-turned parade. There is dancing in the streets. This is known as "the second line," and everyone is welcome. This is a celebration of hope for new life, for the resurrection of the dead.

The grief-stricken walk to the cemetery exists within moments of the joy-infused parade. It's not one or the other, it's both. The grieving is not finished; it is tempered with hope—remembrance that this world does not now, and will not ever, have the final say.

Therefore lift your drooping hands and strengthen your weak

knees, and make straight paths for your feet, so that what is lame may not be put out of joint but rather be healed.

Hebrews 12:12-13

Sitting in the small conference room with this panel of speakers, each sharing the experiences of God's faithful presence in their personal grief, echoed the encouragement of Hebrews 11. In this chapter, the faithfulness of our forefathers is recounted for us as a testimony of God's unfailing commitment to bring forth the promises He has made to His people. Their imperfect surrender stories read like a who's-who of the spiritually elite. Paul names their specific acts of obedience by saying that they stepped into their specific surrender situations by faith:

> By faith Abraham obeyed when he was called to go out to a place that he was to receive as an inheritance (Hebrews 11:8).

> By faith Sarah herself received power to conceive, even when she was past the age, since she considered him faithful who had promised (Hebrews 11:11).

> By faith Isaac invoked future blessings on Jacob and Esau (Hebrews 11:20).

> By faith Jacob, when dying, blessed each of the sons of Joseph, bowing in worship over the head of his staff (Hebrews 11:21).

> By faith Joseph, at the end of his life, made mention of the exodus of the Israelites and gave directions concerning his bones (Hebrews 11:22).

> By faith Moses, when he was born, was hidden for three months by his parents, because they saw that the child was beautiful, and they were not afraid of the king's edict (Hebrews 11:23).

> By faith the people crossed the Red Sea as on dry land, but

the Egyptians, when they attempted to do the same, were drowned (Hebrews 11:29).

By faith the walls of Jericho fell down after they had been encircled for seven days (Hebrews 11:30).

By faith Rahab the prostitute did not perish with those who were disobedient, because she had given a friendly welcome to the spies (Hebrews 11:31).

Paul is only scratching the surface. He says he would run out of time trying to tell all of the stories of the ways God continually made the weak strong for His glory (Hebrews 11:32). This is the best kind of motivational speech, because it takes the pressure off of those who hear. Paul's encouragement centers the full weight of the work on God's shoulders. This cloud of witnesses had faith, but God accomplished His plans through their willingness. And so it is, and will be with our own faithful "yes" to God.

The story isn't over. While death reminds us that we are finite, death is only a comma, not a period. We know that our race ends with the return of the risen Christ, and so while we grieve, we celebrate the hope coming still. We are a people of perpetual hope.

Surprised By Joy

Behold, the dwelling place of God is with man. He will dwell with them, and they will be his people, and God himself will be with them as their God. He will wipe away every tear from their eyes, and death shall be no more, neither shall there be mourning, nor crying, nor pain anymore, for the former things have passed away." And he who was seated on the throne said, "Behold, I am making all things new."

Revelation 21:3-5

This passage from Revelation is read at funerals as a comfort and reminder to those of us who remain with feet pressed into the soil, that our loved ones who have gone on to be with Jesus do not suffer any longer. God speaks the promise of hope for restoration of His creation to those who grieve. Behold, I am making all things new.

Driving home from the conference with the image of the Jazz funeral dancing through my head, it occurred to me how apt the juxtaposition of grief and joy was for my imperfect fast, and the rest of my stumbling attempts at surrender. Whenever God invites me to release something to Him, so often my hand-off is one filled with tears and fears and real grief. But in time, when I have left it to Him, I am always surprised by the joy that emerges. Surrender is a lightening, a shedding that loosens bonds we don't even know are holding us apart from deeper intimacy with God.

A few months ago, I found myself sidelined by an unexpected and major surgery. I'd been suffering for months, and though I suspected it might end this way, I wondered if maybe there was another way to heal. Life is full and I was concerned about the length of the recovery period—how long would I be benched from my routine? In the weeks before the operation, my doctor made it clear that I would need to ask for help. She stressed the critical need to limit my activity, to temper my propensity towards getting stuff done. "You'll need to rest," she said. In her firm warning I heard an invitation to slow down out of necessity (permission I don't easily grant myself). But at the same time, I flinched. I thought Here we go. Another surrender.

If you've sensed anything about my character in this book, it's that slow-mo is not my MO. "If you overdo it, you'll end up back in here," she warned me. In a painful moment of vulnerability, I sent out a text message to a couple of trusted friends and waved my white flag. "I need help. Specifically, I need meals."

Their response was immediate. They each volunteered a dinner for the coming days. Tears leaked down my cheeks as I took in their instant willingness to serve my family. During the next six weeks of recovery, we received daily meals delivered from friends and church members who'd heard about my situation. With the arrival of every new dinner, I couldn't help but be overcome with joy for the generosity of others. This crowd of witnesses encouraged me to rest by serving a real need. Letting go of my usual meal-prep responsibility was not easy. In my less-admirable moments, the surrender I was forced into by the operation felt a little like a prison. Sometimes I grew frustrated by my inability to accomplish the simple, daily tasks I am accustomed to managing for myself. I needed an escort to walk to the bathroom. I needed help getting into my bed. Recovery like this is humbling.

The suddenness of the surgery itself was an answered prayer, but I grieved my limits. Those six weeks of recovery were spent in the recliner in my family room, doing very little. Between the pain medication and my own body's slower functioning as it worked to heal, I could not manage to write. I hadn't anticipated how frustrating I would find this, and how difficult it would be to let go of my expectations of meeting my deadlines.

I thought about this book, and how on earth I could write about surrender when I am clearly, still very much a student in the practice of it. I've debated how I could even end this book, when in some ways I feel as if I am still where I began, still struggling to let God have everything, every part of me. I'm still working out my salvation with fear, trembling and a side of frustration. Surrender is like walking through a labyrinth. At moments you are on the outside edge only to be drawn back towards the center. In and out of the center you weave, closer to God, then further from Him, until at last, you find yourself held totally in His hands. The next time it's familiar—maybe not easier, but at least not so foreign. And the time after that, and the next, you recognize the terrain, you know how it works, you know that eventually, if you keep leaning into God, you'll find yourself held. But there's no conquering it. There's no way to master it—not on this side of the veil.

In my head I hear the words of Saint Benedict, "Always, we begin again." I realize there's a *we* in there. Our surrender journey returns us again and again to what feels like the very place we first began. We begin again—but not exactly where we were. Not precisely.

With every new invitation to let go, we learn a thing or two. The more we surrender, the more reflexive the process becomes. The practice changes our posture. We know a little more about the landscape of God's goodness, a little more about the fruitfulness of wholehearted living. We awake each day to those new mercies David sang about in the Psalms (Psalm 30); We awake to God's steadfast, unconditional love (Lamentations 3:22). We receive with the dawn, God's fresh invitation to offer Him our whole heart for an overflowing portion—the very fullness of God, Himself. Though we may long to "arrive", we accept that we have not— not yet. We'll receive the opportunity to hand our hearts over again with gratitude. Who doesn't love a second, third or fiftieth chance? When we're tempted to slump in defeat, we'll resist in hope. Every new opportunity to surrender, a gentle reminder to live awake to the ways we forget to give it all to Jesus.

Everything is His.

We are His.

And because of His great love, He is ours.

God, You are so near. Though our heart and flesh fail You never stop calling for us to come to You. You see our grief, you take our sadness and You make us new. We don't understand it, but we don't have to. We can lean into Your kindness and trust that because everything is Yours, You are holding it all in far more capable hands than we have. Where we fail, You uphold. Where we stumble, You pick us up. You are merciful without measure. Teach us what it means to be willing to be willing. Teach us to say "yes" with our spirit, when our lips feel too dry and cracked to part. In our stubbornness Lord, meet us gently, and lead us into the freedom of loving You with all that we are. In Your abundant and most patient love, hear our prayer.
In Jesus' name, Amen.

NOTES

CHAPTER 1— COMFORTABLE DECEPTIONS

1. Michel, Jen Pollock. *Teach Us to Want: Longing, Ambition and the Life if Faith.* Ivp Books, 2016.

2. Sorge, Bob. *Secrets of the Secret Place: Keys to Igniting Your Personal Time with God.* Oasis House, 2001.

3. Fénelon, François de Salignac de La Mothe-. *The Seeking Heart: Including a Short Biography.* Seed Sowers, 1992.

4. Buchanan, Mark. *The Holy Wild: Trusting in the Character of God.* Multnomah Books, 2005.

5. Manning, Brennan. *The Ragamuffin Gospel: Good news for the Bedraggled, Beat-Up, and Burnt Out.* Multnomah Books, 2015.

6. Barna, George. *Maximum Faith: Live Like Jesus, Experience Genuine Transformation.* Brentwood, TN: Published in association with the literary agency of Fedd & Co., 2011.

7. Murray, Andrew. *Absolute Surrender. Addresses Delivered in England and Scotland.* 1899.

CHAPTER 2— HOW MUCH DOES IT COST?

1. Swindoll, Charles R. *Intimacy with the Almighty: Encountering Christ in the Secret Places of Your Life* (17). Word, 1996.

2. Thompson, Francis, and Stella Langdale. *The Hound of Heaven.* Dodd, Mead, 1922.

3. Bonhoeffer, Dietrich. *The Cost of Discipleship.* Macmillan, 1959.

4. http://www.hymnary.org/text/i_hear_the_savior_say_thy_strength_indee

5. Swindoll, Charles R. *Intimacy with the Almighty: Encountering Christ in the Secret Places of Your Life* (67). Word, 1996.

CHAPTER 3— PRESCRIBED BURNS

1. Daigle, Lauren. "Once and For All." Genius. Accessed September 26, 2019. //genius.com/Lauren-daigle-once-and-for-all-lyrics

2. https://www.nature.org/en-us/about-us/where-we-work/united-states/florida/stories-in-florida/florida-restoring-fire-to-native-landscapes/">https://www.nature.org/en-us/about-us/where-we-work/united-states/florida/stories-in-florida/florida-restoring-fire-to-native-landscapes/

3. Buchannan, Mark, The Holy Wild: Trusting in the Character of God. Multnomah Books, 2003.

4. Buchannan, Mark, The Holy Wild: Trusting in the Character of God. Multnomah Books, 2003.

5. https://www.thegospelcoalition.org/article/jabez-and-the-soft-prosperity-gospel1/

6. Reynolds, Rebecca, Courage Dear Heart: Letters To A Weary World. Navpress, 2018

7. Trotter, Isabella Lilias. Parables of the Cross, by I. Lilias Trotter. London: Marshall Brothers, 1900.

CHAPTER 4— I AM THE ISRAELITES

1. Tozer, A.W. Knowledge of the Holy. Harper Collins, 1978.

2. Lewis, C.S. The Weight of Glory. Macmillan, 1949.

3. Taylor, Barbara Brown, Learning To Walk In The Dark. Harper One, 2014.

4. Taylor, Barbara Brown, Learning To Walk In The Dark. Harper One, 2014.

CHAPTER 5— SELAH

1. https://www.amusingplanet.com/2014/07/shrek-sheep-who-escaped-shearing-for-6.html?m=1

2. http://news.bbc.co.uk/2/hi/europe/4665511.stm

3. Elliot, Elisabeth. *A Lamp For My Feet*. Servant Publications, 1987.

4. Peterson, Eugene H. *A Long Obedience in the Same Direction: Discipleship in an Instant Society.* InterVarsity Press, 1980.

5. Brother Lawrence, *The Practice Of The Presence of God*. Image Books, 1977

CHAPTER 6— TEN MILES FOR MANI

1. Flannery O'Connor, *The Habit of Being: Letters of Flannery O'Connor.* Farrar, Straus and Giroux, 1988

2. Acuff, Jon. *Finish: Give Yourself the Gift of Done*. Portfolio, 2017

3. Murray, Andrew. *Absolute Surrender: And Other Addresses.* Merchant Books, 2012

CHAPTER 7— YOU'RE NOT THE ONLY ONE

1. Barton, Ruth Haley. *Strengthening The Soul of Your Leadership: Seeking God In The Crucible Of Ministry.* IVP, 2018

2. Buechner, Frederick. *Wishful Thinking: A Theological ABC.* Harper & Row, 1973.

CHAPTER 8— YOU CAN'T ALWAYS GET WHAT YOU   WANT

1. Cohen, Leonard. "Anthem". Genius. Accessed September 27, 2019. // *genius.com/Leonard-cohen-anthem-lyrics*

2. Wolf, Lanny. "Surely the Presence of the Lord is in This Place". Share Faith. Accessed September 27, 2019. // *sharefaith.com/guide/Christian-Music/Hymns/Presence-of-the-lord*

3. Tolkien, J.R.R. *The Fellowship of the Ring*. Houghton Mifflin Harcourt, 2014.

4. Job 1:21, KJV

5. Murray, Andrew. *Prayer Life*. Wilder Publications, 2018.

CHAPTER 9— STRUCK DOWN BUT NOT DESTROYED

1. Buechner, Frederick. *A Crazy, Holy Grace The Healing Power of Pain and Memory.* Abingdon Pr, 2018.

2. Lewis, Clive S. *The Problem of Pain.* HarperCollins, 2014.

3. Lewis, Clive S. *The Problem of Pain.* HarperCollins, 2014.

4. Buchannan, Mark, *The Holy Wild: Trusting in the Character of God.* Multnomah Books, 2003

5. Buechner, Frederick. *A Crazy, Holy Grace The Healing Power of Pain and Memory.* Abingdon Pr, 2018.

6. Buechner, Frederick. *A Crazy, Holy Grace The Healing Power of Pain and Memory.* Abingdon Pr, 2018.

7. Ten Boom, Corrie. *The Hiding Place.* Chosen Books. 2006

8. *href="https://mymodernmet.com/kintsugi-kintsukuroi/)">https://mymodernmet.com/kintsugi-kintsukuroi/)*

9. Eric Roth, *The Curious Case of Benjamin Button,* Screenplay

CHAPTER 10— ALL THINGS NEW

1. Carolyn Arends, *Hutchmoot.* Nashville, TN. 2019 (Learn more about this at Hutchmoot.com and then make this your pilgrimage—even if only once before you die.)

2. Roseveare, Helen. *Living Sacrifice: Willing to be Whittled as an Arrow.* Ross-shire, Great Britain: Christian Focus Pub., 2007.

With Thanks...

So many friends and strangers have encouraged and supported me in the effort to bring this book from my head and heart to the page. I am astounded at the ways and means God takes to encourage our hearts when we are most desperately in need, and I have never felt more desperate than the seasons spent (so far) walking through this message in my actual life.

Jesus: I thank you first because you first loved me, and you love me still, even as I stagger and stumble my way to you in surrender. As hard as it is and as much as I resist, you keep holding out your arms to me, and I get to re-learn what it is to live in the bottomless well of your kindness, mercy and grace. Never let me go, no matter how tight I may close my hands to you, keep me close and teach me again and again the gift of letting you have my whole heart. Bind my wandering heart to thee.

Kurt: Nobody has to endure my angst the way that you do. You are a steady pillar of unrelenting love in my life, and I am ever grateful. Thank you for helping me manage all of the things while I juggle book writing, homeschooling and retreat hosting. Thank you for talking me off of the ledges I'm so quick to scramble up onto, and for being a source of encouragement and wisdom. I love you more than I can express here, and thank God for you.

Luke, Sam, Abby, and Phoebe: You four are the most beautiful gift that God has given me, and the means by which He repeatedly teaches me what it looks like to surrender. Thank you for loving me so generously, even when I'm lost in writing and forget to make you lunch, and arrive on time (too early) to all of the places. I love you all so much, and Jesus loves you even more—which is so hard to imagine, and still, entirely true.

Seana: Thank you for trusting me with the tender fragments of your story. I carry you with me, always.

Christin Ditchfield, Robin Dance, Elizabeth Marshall, Susan Mulder, Jennifer Lee, Michelle DeRusha: You ladies are gold to me. I can't thank you enough for enduring draft after draft, and conversation after conversation about this project over the years, for your prayers and hand-holding along the way. I am confident that without your prayers and encouragement, I'd still be trying to untangle the knots of this book in my head.

Christine Hiester: Your support and prayerful guidance in my life and over this project is a generosity from the very hands of God. Your unfailing friendship and gentle voice of wisdom is a treasure I hold close to my heart. Thank you for demonstrating for me, the mercy of God and for teaching me to pray in new ways. And your art! I am forever indebted to you for sharing your gifts with me. I love you.

Lancia E. Smith: Your voice is often in my head speaking kind words of encouragement to me when I am in a hole of doubt and discouragement. Your mentorship and friendship are a gift I treasure. Thank you for the way you cultivate beauty in the lives of so many, and most especially, in my life.

Jeanine: Your optimism, steady cheerleading and friendship are a gift. I love you.

The women of Refine {the retreat}: You are my people. Your camaraderie and encouragement over the years is an ebeneezer of God's goodness that I return to again and again. I can never fully express what your notes and letters and friendship has meant to me except to offer this small and insufficient word of gratitude. Your showing up year after year on retreat with me leads me deeper into the heart of Jesus.

Christa Wells and Taylor Leonhardt: Thank you for the very specific words you spoke to me on the lawn at Refine in 2019, and for the ways you mentor me with your art and songs and lives. You show me Jesus every day.

Jeff Braun: Thank you for the time and care you took to nudge me forward in this work. Your encouragement in the early days of this project was a gift.

Ruth Samsel: Thank you for teaching me a few things I didn't know and for giving me so much of your time and encouragement. I am grateful for the season of working with you.

John Blase: I never imagined that I'd get to work with you all those years ago when I found you through Brennan Manning's work, but this full-circle experience is a God-wink to me. Years ago, you were there when that particular book tipped me into the bottomless waters of God's grace, and to walk this leg of my journey alongside you in this work, has been proof that God weaves the best stories, and then has the audacity to let us live them. I am confident that I would not have finished this project without your help, encouragement and sharp editing skills. Your work in these pages is a gift to me, and to the readers who work their way through these chapters. Thank you for believing in this message and project and for always shooting straight with me. I am deeply grateful.

About The Author

Kris is the author of, *Come Lord Jesus: The Weight Of Waiting,* and *Holey, Wholly, Holy: A Lenten Journey of Refinement.* In addition to contributing to multiple books, her writing has also been featured on numerous websites. She is the founder and director of *Refine {the retreat}*, a yearly Christian Women's retreat in Ohio. In her free time, she writes at kriscamealy.com.

Also By Kris Camealy

Finding Church: Stories of Finding, Switching, and Reforming (Civitas Press, 2012)

Holey, Wholly, Holy: A Lenten Journey Of refinement (Create Space 2013)

Come Lord Jesus: The Weight Of Waiting (Create Space, 2016)

Soul Bare: Stories of Redemption (Contributor, IVP, 2016)

Craving Connection: 30 Challenges For real Life Engagement (Contributor, B&H Books, 2017)

The Heart of Marriage: Stories That Celebrate The Adventure Of Life Together (Contributor, Revell, 2017)

A Moment To Breathe: 365 Devotions That meet You in Your Everyday (Contributor, B&H Publisher, 2017)

CSB (In)Courage Devotional Bible, (Contributor, B&H Publishing, 2018)

Made in the USA
Columbia, SC
30 May 2020